Excel Skills Boost

Excel Skills Boost

First Edition, 2017

Russell Templar Ltd.
Registered in England and Wales
Company Number: 10187229

www.russelltemplar.com

ISBN-13: 978-1976275715

ISBN-10: 1976275717

About the Author

I have worked in the IT and financial fields since 1997. I have many years' experience as a software developer and I am also a chartered accountant. In my experience in both the IT and financial fields, Excel has always been one of the main software packages used. I started using spreadsheets before my computer came with a mouse. When I started using spreadsheets the software was called Lotus 1-2-3 and together with WordPerfect, you could "run" an office. Over the years my skills grew with the various versions of Excel that was released. I qualified as a chartered accountant in 2010 at one of the big four audit firms where I was also introduced to the world of training. I quickly realised that I seemed to work quicker and more efficient in Excel than most of my colleagues. This was not because my colleagues did not have IT skills or were new to Excel. They just needed to be shown certain skills and techniques to sharpen their skill they already had. From that need came this book, that I originally used as a training manual for a one-day Excel course.

I moved to the UK in 2013 and have been working in the financial field here as well and saw the same need for the training here. Although it is currently not practical for me to run full-time training courses I have decided to publish this book.

Anton, 2017
First Edition

For Janine …

Contents

Background 1

    Downloads 1

Before we begin.. 2

    The Ribbon 2

    Shortcut keys 3

    Cell selection notation 3

    Material.. 3

    Excel layout 3

    End of Exercises... 5

Working with cells and worksheets 7

    Selecting adjacent multiple cells 7

    Selecting non-adjacent multiple cells 7

    Selecting all cells in a worksheet 7

    Merge adjacent cells 8

    Split a merged cell 8

    Find merged cells 9

    Inserting a Worksheet 10

    Deleting a Worksheet 11

    Copy a Worksheet 12

    Move a Worksheet.. 13

    Renaming a Worksheet 14

    Navigating Worksheets 15

    Select Worksheets in a Range.. 16

    Select Non-Adjacent Worksheets 16

    Select all Worksheets 16

Exercise: Working with cells and worksheets 17

Worksheet Protection 18

    Unlock Cells.. 18

    Protect the Worksheet 21

    Unprotect the Worksheet 21

Exercise: Worksheet protection 22

Paste Special 23

Exercise: Paste Special 26

Nesting Functions 28

    Insert a Function within a Function 28

Absolute Referencing 30

Exercise: Absolute Referencing 31

Logical Functions 32

    IF Function 32

    AND Function 35

    OR Function 37

    IFERROR Function 39

Exercise: Logical Functions 40

VLOOKUP Function 44

Exercise: VLOOKUP Function 48

Named Ranges 49

    Naming a Cell 49

    Using Column Headings to Name Columns 49

    Manually create a Name from a Selected Range 50

    Insert a Named Range in Formulas 50

    Editing a Named Range 51

    Navigating Named Ranges 53

Exercise: Named Ranges 54

Mathematical Functions 56

    SUMIF Function 56

    AVERAGEIF Function 59

Exercise: SUMIF Function 61

Conditional Formatting 62

    Add Conditional Formatting 62

    Add Conditional Formatting across Rows 63

    Copy Conditional Formatting 64

    Change Conditional Formatting 65

    Remove Conditional Formatting 65

    Highlight Duplicates 65

Exercise: Conditional Formatting 66

Auditing a Formula 68

   Trace Precedent/Dependent Arrows 68

   Remove Arrows 69

Exercise: Auditing a Formula 70

PivotTables 73

   Concept and Layout..75

   PivotTable Field List 76

   Turn the Field List On/Off...76

   PivotTable Ribbon 77

   PivotTable Layout 77

   Create a PivotTable 79

   Format a PivotTable 81

   Remove/Add and Move Fields 82

   Remove a Field 82

   Add a Field 83

   Move Fields within the Table..83

   Changes to Source Data..84

   Filter a PivotTable Report 84

   Field Settings in Row/Column Labels...85

   Create a Custom Name 86

   Value Field Settings in Values 88

   Change Number Format 88

   Data Drill Down..89

   Calculated Fields 90

   Edit/Delete calculated field...92

   Changes to the Location/Area of the Source Data 92

Exercise: PivotTables..94

Hyperlinks 97

Exercise: Hyperlinks 98

Text Functions..99

   LEFT Function 99

   MID Function 102

   FIND Function 103

   CONCATENATE Function 106

   TRIM Function 108

LEN Function 109

TEXT Function 110

Exercise: Text Functions 111

Working with Data Lists 115

Sorting Data 116

Single Level Sorting 116

Multi-Level Sorting 117

Set a Custom Sort Order 117

Sorting data by Rows 121

Exercise: Sorting Data 123

Exercise: Custom Sort order 126

Subtotalling 129

Create Subtotals 129

Remove all Subtotals 130

Copying Subtotals 130

Exercise: Subtotalling 132

SUBTOTAL Function 135

Filtering Data 138

Filter Options 139

Apply AutoFilter 141

Clear Filter 143

Remove AutoFilter 143

Advanced Filter Features 144

Exercise: Filtering Data 145

Exercise: Advanced Filtering 147

Group and Outline 149

Group rows and Columns 149

Ungroup Parts of the Outline 149

Remove an Outline 150

Exercise: Group and Outline 151

Working with Charts 153

Creating a Chart 153

Design Tab 154

Layout Tab 154

Format Tab 154

Changing the Chart Type 155

Changing the Location of a Chart 156

Edit Chart Labels 156

Specifying your own Series 156

Creating a Chart with Two Independent axes 159

Exercise: Working with Charts 162

Exercise: Dual Axes 163

Using comments 165

Add a comment 165

Edit a comment 166

Delete a comment 166

Display or hide comments on the worksheet 167

Display or hide all comments on the worksheet 167

Exercise: Using Comments 168

Data Validation 169

Restrict data entry to values in a drop-down list 170

Select an Input message for the Data Validation 172

Select an Error Alert for the Data Validation 174

Exercise: Data Validation 175

Goal Seek 176

Exercise: Goal Seek 178

Macros 179

Record a Macro 179

Run, Edit or Delete a Macro 180

Assign a macro to an object, graphic, or control 181

Relative Macro 181

Assign Macros to the Quick Access Toolbar 183

Exercise: Macros 186

Excel Keyboard Shortcuts - Ctrl combination shortcut keys 190

Excel Keyboard Shortcuts - Function keys 192

Excel Keyboard Shortcuts - Miscellaneous 194

Background

I have worked in the IT, audit and accounting fields and presented Excel courses for financial staff for the last few years. I have noticed that a lot of long-time Excel users are only scratching the surface of what is possible. By raising your skills, even marginally, you will be exponentially more efficient with your spreadsheets.

If you had to compare this book with most generic Excel courses out there I would place it between intermediate and advanced. This book is aimed at users with an established Excel understanding. Most everyday users of Excel can benefit from this book.

In my experience, a day of intense focus is needed for this book. I would suggest tackling one topic at a time, including the exercises.

This book was originally written with Excel 2010 in mind. It was updated for Excel 2013 with no change to the content, just the screen shots changed. As this book is aimed at fundamental techniques in Excel it is still applicable even with Excel 2016.

This book comes with exercises and solutions. These can be downloaded at the link provided below. You can download the exercises and solutions before you start the book. This book is aimed at adult learners and caters for different styles of learning. It is recommended to only reference the solutions after at least attempting the exercises first.

Downloads

You can download the exercises and solutions at:

www.russelltemplar.com/books

Before we begin...

The Ribbon

The menu in Excel is referred to as a **ribbon**. A ribbon is divided into **Tabs**, **Groups**, and **Buttons**, the reason for this ribbon is efficiency. You should be able to perform most tasks in Excel in only two clicks.

In the exercises in this book, if you need to click on the **Cut** button it will be displayed as:

Click [**Home**][**Clipboard**][**Cut**]

Some of the buttons have multiple options if you click on them, in those cases, there will be more square brackets e.g.:

Click [**Home**][**Styles**][**Conditional Formatting**][**Highlight Cells Rules**][**Duplicate Values...**]

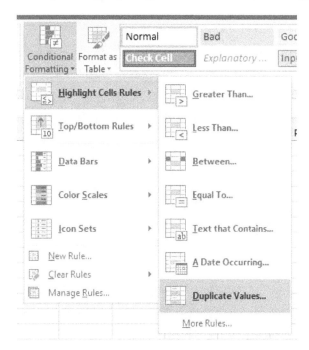

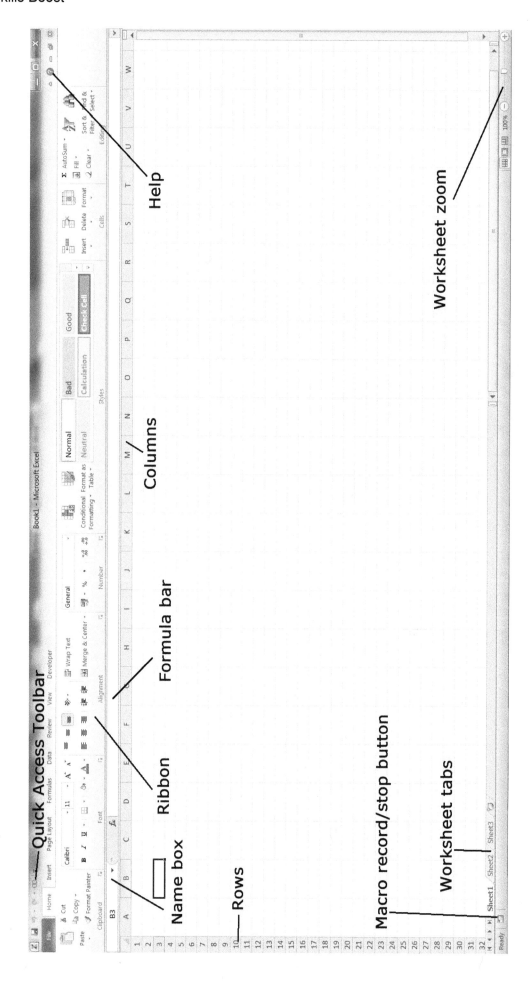

In Excel 2016 the help can be found at the end of the tabs in the ribbon.

End of Exercises

None of the exercises in this book explains to you what to do once you have completed an exercise. That will be up to you. You can either save to file or not. Remember you can always get the clean exercises from the internet or you can make a copy of them before you start, in case you want to redo any of them.

Working with cells and worksheets

Selecting cells

Selecting adjacent multiple cells

Method

1. Click on the first cell and hold the left mouse button down
2. **Drag** the mouse over all the cells you want to select
3. Release the mouse button

OR

1. Select the first cell by clicking in it
2. Move the worksheet so that the cell that will encapsulate all the data is visible
3. Press and hold **Shift**
4. Click the cell that encapsulates all the data
5. Release **Shift**

Selecting non-adjacent multiple cells

Method

1. Select the first cell by clicking in it
2. Press on hold the **Ctrl** button
3. Now select all the cells you want to select
4. Release the **Ctrl** button

Selecting all cells in a worksheet

1. Click the **Select All** button

Select All button

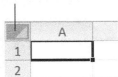

OR

1. Press **Ctrl + A**

> **Shortcut:** If the worksheet contains data, and the active cell is above or to the left of the data, pressing **Ctrl+A** selects the current region. Pressing **Ctrl+A** a second time selects the entire worksheet.

Merge and unmerge cells

When you merge two or more adjacent horizontal or vertical cells, the cells become one larger cell that is displayed across multiple columns or rows. When you merge multiple cells, the contents of only one cell (the upper-left cell) appear in the merged cell. The contents of the other cells that you merge are deleted. After merging cells, you can split a merged cell into separate cells again. If you don't remember where you have merged cells, you can use the Find command to quickly locate merged cells.

Merge adjacent cells

Method

1. **Select** two or more adjacent cells that you want to merge

   Note: Make sure that the data that you want to display in the merged cell is contained in the upper-left cell of the selected range. Only the data in the upper-left cell will remain in the merged cell. Data in all the other cells of the selected range will be deleted. Copy any other data you need to another location on the worksheet before merging.

2. On the **Home** tab, in the **Alignment** group, click **Merge and Center**

   The cells will be merged in a row or column, and the cell contents will be centred in the merged cell. To merge cells without centring, click the arrow next to **Merge and Center**, and then click **Merge Across** or **Merge Cells**.

3. To change the text alignment in the merged cell, select the cell, and then click any of the alignment buttons in the **Alignment** group on the **Home** tab

Split a merged cell

Method

1. **Select** the merged cell that you want to unmerge
2. To split the merged cell, click **Merge and Center**, or click the arrow next to **Merge and Center**, and then click **Unmerge Cells**

   Immediately after merging cells, you can also unmerge them by clicking **Undo** on the **Quick Access Toolbar**, or by pressing **CTRL+Z**

3. The contents of the merged cell will appear in the upper-left cell of the range of split cells

Find merged cells

Method

1. On the **Home** tab, in the **Editing** group, click **Find & Select**

2. Click **Find**
3. On the **Find** tab, click **Options**, and then click **Format**

   Note: If you don't see the **Format** button, click **Options**

4. On the **Alignment** tab, under **Text control**, select the **Merge cells** check box, and then click **OK**
5. Do one of the following:

   - To find the next occurrence of a merged cell, click **Find Next**

   Excel selects the next merged cell on the worksheet

   - To find all merged cells, click **Find All**

   Excel displays a list of all merged cells in the bottom section of the **Find and Replace** dialog box. When you select a merged cell in this list, Excel selects that merged cell on the worksheet

---

Note: Formula references in other cells are adjusted automatically to use the cell reference of the merged cell.

Because sorting requires that all cells to be sorted are using the same size, you **cannot sort a range that contains** a combination of **merged** and unmerged cells.

Inserting a Worksheet

Method

1. Click the **Insert Worksheet** tab at the bottom of the screen

OR

1. To insert a new worksheet in front of an existing worksheet
2. Select that worksheet
3. On the **Home** tab, in the **Cells** group, click **Insert**, and then click **Insert Sheet**

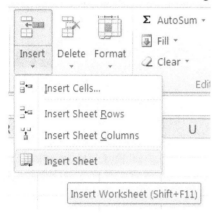

OR

1. **Right** click the tab of an existing worksheet
2. Click **Insert**
3. On the **General** tab, click **Worksheet**
4. Click **OK**

OR

1. Press **Shift + F11**

Short cut: *To add a new worksheet press - **Shift + F11***

Deleting a Worksheet

Method

1. **Right** click on the **worksheet tab** you want to delete
2. From the **Shortcut** menu, select **Delete**
3. Select **OK**

OR

1. Select the **worksheet** or worksheets that you want to delete.
2. On the **Home** tab, in the **Cells** group, click the arrow next to **Delete**, and then click **Delete Sheet**

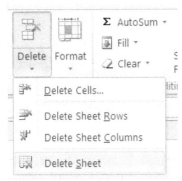

> ***Beware***: *Once you have deleted a Worksheet in Excel you will not be able to undo your action.*

Copy a Worksheet

Using the mouse

<u>Method</u>

1. Press and hold **Ctrl**
2. **Drag** the worksheet tab of the worksheet you want to copy to its new location, releasing the mouse button when the black triangle is in the desired location
3. Release **Ctrl**

Shortcut Menu

<u>Method</u>

1. **Right** click the tab of the worksheet you want to copy
2. From the **Shortcut** menu, select **Move or Copy...**

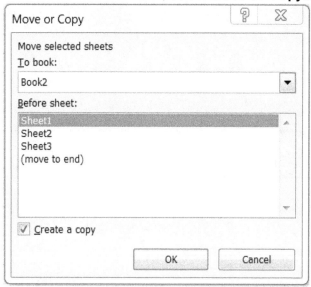

3. In the **Move or Copy** dialog box, from the **To Book** drop-down list, select the desired workbook
4. In the **Before Sheet** list box, select the worksheet before which the copied worksheet will appear
5. Select the **Create a Copy** check box
6. Select **OK**

Move a Worksheet

Using the mouse

Method

1. **Drag** the worksheet tab of the worksheet to its new location, releasing the mouse button when the black triangle is in the desired location

Shortcut Menu

Method

1. **Right** click the tab of the worksheet you want to copy
2. From the **Shortcut** menu, select **Move or Copy...**

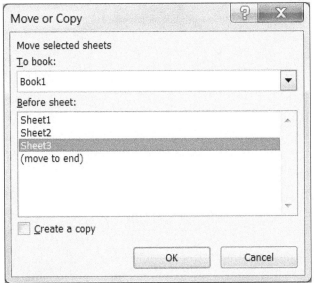

3. In the **Move or Copy** dialog box, from the **To Book** drop-down list, select the desired workbook
4. In the **Before Sheet** list box, select the worksheet before which the selected worksheet will appear
5. Select **OK**

Note: When you need to view more than one workbook at a time:

> *On the **View** tab, the **Window** group, select **Arrange All***

> *Select **Tile** or **Vertical***

*This is also useful for **Copying** or **Moving** worksheets*

Renaming a Worksheet

You can rename any worksheet in an Excel workbook. The name can be up to 31 characters long and cannot contain the following characters : ( ) / \ ? *

Method

1. On the **Sheet tab** bar, **right** click the sheet tab that you want to rename, and then click **Rename**

Active Sheet

2. Enter the new name
3. Press **Enter**

OR

1. On the **Sheet tab** bar, double click on sheet tab that you want to rename

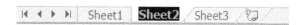

2. Enter the new name
3. Click anywhere on the sheet to continue

Navigating Worksheets

Method

1. **Right** click on the **worksheet navigation arrows**

Worksheet Navigation Arrows

2. Select the **worksheet** you want to navigate to

> **Short cut:** You can also Press **Ctrl & Page Up** or **Page Down** to navigate to the next or previous worksheet

Grouping Worksheets

By grouping worksheets, you are able to apply certain formatting and formulas to multiple worksheets. This can save a great amount of time. The only requirement is that the region in which you wish to make modifications across the grouped worksheets needs to be set out in the same format.

Select Worksheets in a Range

Method

1. Select the **first** worksheet
2. Hold down **Shift** and select the **last** worksheet of the range
3. To deselect, select a worksheet that has **NOT** been selected

Select Non-Adjacent Worksheets

Method

1. Select the first worksheet
2. Hold down **Ctrl** and select the additional worksheets
3. To deselect, select a worksheet that has **NOT** been selected

Select all Worksheets

Method

1. **Right** click on any worksheet tabs, select, **Select All Sheets**
2. To de-select, **right** click on any of the worksheet tabs and select **Ungroup sheets**

> You can **always** de-select grouped worksheets by **right** clicking the worksheet **tabs** and selecting **Ungroup sheets**, no matter how you grouped them.

Exercise: Working with cells and worksheets

Open file: **Working with cells and worksheets.xlsx**

Steps

- Insert **five** new worksheets to the workbook
- Select **Sheet 1**
- Select range (B2:C2)
- Click on [**Home**][**Alignment**][**Merge & Center**]
- Rename **Sheet 1** to **First**
- **Copy** the **First** worksheet twice
- Rename the new worksheets **Second** and **Third** and **move** them into order
- Select the merged cell **B2** on **Second**. Change it to **My Sheet 2**
- Select the merged cell **B2** on **Third**. Change it to **My Sheet 3**
- Delete worksheets **Sheet 2** and **Sheet 3**
- Select worksheet **First**
- Hold **Ctrl** and select the worksheet **tabs** for worksheets **Second** and **Third**
- Select the merged cell **B2** on the **First** worksheet
- Change the **format** to **red** text, **yellow** highlight and a **frame**
- If you now look at the **Second** and **Third** worksheets the formatting of **B2** should be the same as in the **First** worksheet

Solution

Shortcut keys

In this book, there are **shortcut keys** for many of the functions e.g. **Ctrl+C** for **Copy** and **Ctrl+V** for **Paste**. These shortcuts make it more effective to perform certain tasks. At the back of this book, you will find a comprehensive list of shortcuts you could use in Excel.

Cell selection notation

Cells are referred to by their **column letter** or **row number**: **B2** will be the **second** cell in column **B**.

In this book, you often have to select **multiple** cells. When you have to select cells **B2:D9** (with the **:** in between) you need to select all the cells that **encompass** those references.

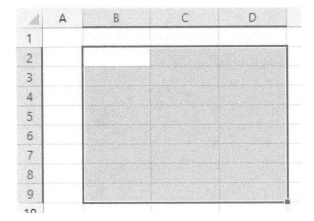

Material

You can download the exercises and solutions at:

www.russelltemplar.com/books

Excel layout

On the next page, you will find a screenshot of Excel with some areas identified

Worksheet Protection

To prevent a user from accidentally or deliberately changing, moving, or deleting important data from a worksheet or workbook, you can protect certain worksheet or workbook elements, with or without a password. You can remove the protection from a worksheet as needed.

> *When protecting the worksheet, you must **first** unlock the cells that you want to **edit** and then protect the worksheet*
>
> *To ensure the person using the worksheet cannot copy the data and paste it to another workbook you must de-select "**Select locked cells**" in the **Protection** dialog box.*

Unlock Cells

The cells that you unlock are the cells that you will be able to edit after protecting the worksheet.

Method

1. Select the **cells**, **columns** or **rows** that can be edited
2. From the **Home** tab, in the **Cells** group select **Format**

3. Select **Lock Cell** from the list

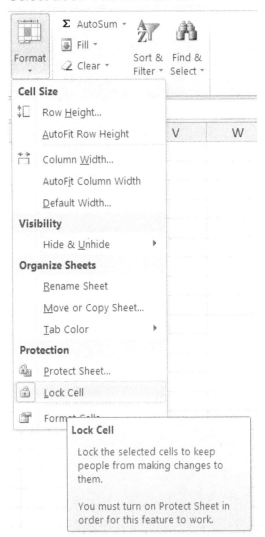

The icon does not change; you either **select** it or **deselect** it by clicking on it

OR

1. Select the **cells**, **columns** or **rows** that can be edited
2. Right click and select **Format Cells...**

3. On the **Format Cells** dialog box select the **Protection** tab

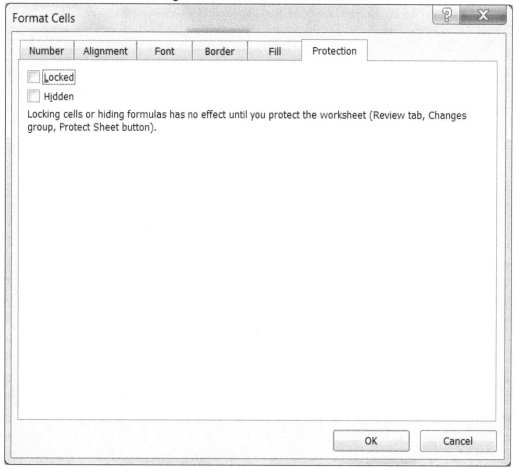

4. **Deselect** the **Locked** option
5. Click on **OK**

Note: You can **Lock** the cells again by following the steps above.

Protect the Worksheet

Method

1. From the **Home** tab, in the **Cells** group, select **Format**
2. Select **Protect Sheet** from the list

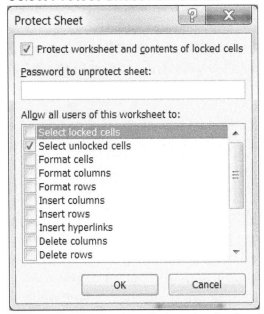

3. Ensure you de-select **Select locked cells**
   This will ensure the worksheet cannot be copied and pasted
4. Enter a **password** or leave blank
5. Select **OK**

Unprotect the Worksheet

Method

1. From the **Home** tab, in the **Cells** group, select **Format**
2. Select **Unprotect Sheet** from the list
3. Enter the **password** if necessary
4. Select **OK**

---

*Note: You can also **right** click the worksheet tab and **Protect/Unprotect** your worksheets.*

Exercise: Worksheet protection

Open file: ***Worksheet protection.xlsx***

<u>Steps</u>

- Select the yellow, highlighted **Section A** on the **Sections** worksheet (**D4:D19**)
- Click on [**Home**][**Cells**][**Format**][**Lock Cell**]
- Click on [**Home**][**Cells**][**Format**][**Protect Sheet**]
- Make sure only the **Select unlocked cells** option is selected. **Don't enter a password**
- Now you should only be able to enter information into the yellow highlighted **Section A**

- Click on [**Home**][**Cells**][**Format**][**Unprotect Sheet**]
- The sheet will now be **unprotected** again
- Select the yellow, highlighted **Section A** on the Sections Worksheet (**D4:D19**)
- Click on [**Home**][**Cells**][**Format**][**Lock Cell**]
- Select the green highlighted **Section B** on the Sections Worksheet (**G4:G19**)
- Click on [**Home**][**Cells**][**Format**][**Lock Cell**]
- Click on [**Home**][**Cells**][**Format**][**Protect Sheet**]
- Make sure only the **Select unlocked cells** option is selected. **Don't enter a password**
- Now you should only be able to enter information into the green highlighted **Section B**

Paste Special

Using the **Paste Special** dialog box when pasting your copied data, you have the option to select specific contents of the copied data, which you would like to paste in the destination area, including options to do mathematical calculations, not replacing blank copied cells and transposing the data.

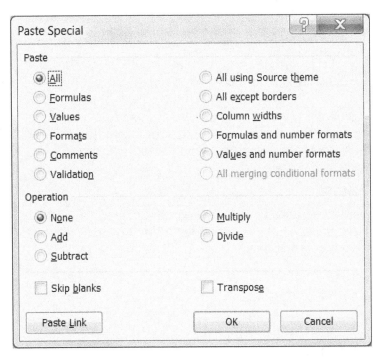

PASTE	
All	Paste all the stuff in the cell selection (formulas, formatting, etc.). This is what happens when you paste normally.
Formulas	Paste all the text, numbers, and formulas in the current cell selection without their formatting.
Values	Convert formulas in the current cell selection to their calculated values.
Formats	Paste only the formatting from the current cell selection, without the cell entries.
Comments	Paste only the notes that you attach to their cells (like electronic post-it notes).
Validation	Paste only the data validation rules into the cell range that you set up with the Data Validation command.
All using Source theme	Paste all the information plus the cell styles applied to the cells.
All except borders	Paste all the stuff in the cell selection without copying any borders you use there.
Column widths	Apply the column widths of the cells copied to the Clipboard to the columns where the cells are pasted.
Formulas and number formats	Include the number formats assigned to the pasted values and formulas.
Values and number formats	Convert formulas to their calculated values and include the number formats you assigned to all the copied or cut values.

All merging conditional formats	Paste conditional formatting into the cell range.
OPERATION	
None	Excel performs no operation between the data entries you cut or copy to the Clipboard and the data entries in the cell range where you paste. This is the default setting.
Add/subtract etc.	Excel adds, subtracts, multiplies or divides the values you cut or copy to the Clipboard to the values in the cell range where you paste.
Skip blanks	Select this check box when you want Excel to paste only from the cells that aren't empty.
Transpose	Select this check box when you want Excel to change the orientation of the pasted entries. For example, if the original cells' entries run down the rows of a single column of the worksheet, the transposed pasted entries will run across the columns of a single row.
PASTE LINK	
Paste Link	Click this button when you want to establish a link between the copies you're pasting and the original entries. That way, changes to the original cells automatically update in the pasted copies.

Method

1. Select the cells/range you want to copy
2. From the **Home** tab, in the **Clipboard** group, select **Copy**
3. Select the destination cell
4. From the **Home** tab, in the **Clipboard** group, select the **drop-down** arrow under **Paste**
5. Select **Paste Special...**

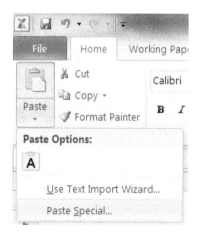

6. Make your selection as stated above
7. Click **OK**

OR

1. Select the cells/range you want to copy.

2. Press **Ctrl & C**
3. Select the destination cell
4. **Right click** your mouse

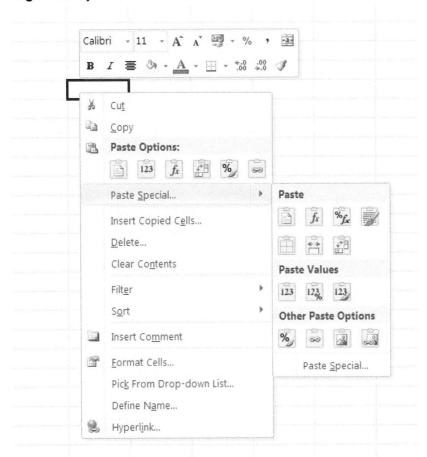

5. Either click on **Paste Special** to bring up dialog box or select one of the **icons** that represent you option

---

Short cuts: You can use *Ctrl & C* to *Copy*, *Ctrl & X* to *Cut*, *Ctrl & V* to *Paste* and *Ctrl & Alt & V* to bring up the *Paste Special* dialog box.

Exercise: Paste Special

Open file: *Paste Special.xlsx*

On the **West** worksheet

Steps

- Select the data on the **West** worksheet (**A1:J5**)
- **Copy** the data
- Select cell **A1** on the **New West** worksheet
- Use **Paste Special** and **Transpose** the paste the data here
- The data in **New West** worksheet should now look the same as the data on **East** worksheet

On the **Combined** worksheet

Steps

- Select the data on the **New West** worksheet (**A2:E10**) (**Do not copy the heading in Row1**)
- **Copy** the data
- Select cell **A2** on the **Combined** worksheet
- Use **Paste Special** and **Paste Link** to paste the data here
- The data in **Combined** should now look the same as the data on **New West**
- Select the data on the **East** worksheet (**A2:E19**) (**Do not copy the heading in Row1**)
- **Copy** the data
- Select cell **A11** on the **Combined** worksheet
- Use **Paste Special** and **Paste Link** to paste the data here
- The data in **Combined** should now look the same as the data on **New West** as well as **East**
- If you now **change** any on the data lines on **New West** or **East**, you should see that **change** reflected on the **Combined** worksheet

Solution

New West worksheet

	A	B	C	D	E
1	**Name**	**Surname**	**Invoice Number**	**Amount Incl VAT**	**Amount Excl VAT**
2	Billie	Moss	INV 1961045	202 347.06	177 497.42
3	Katharine	Lucas	INV 1072780	1 129 082.29	990 423.06
4	Lester	Rich	INV 1390667	369 630.67	324 237.43
5	Johnny	Carlton	INV 1985138	1 026 695.14	900 609.77
6	Ashley	Brady	INV 1593852	875 287.97	767 796.46
7	Lauren	Schultz	INV 1939541	1 440 353.78	1 263 468.23
8	Carolyn	Nichols	INV 1488644	380 303.93	333 599.94
9	Louis	Harvey	INV 1579705	439 607.48	385 620.60
10	Charlene	Stevenson	INV 1857410	157 204.90	137 899.04

Combined worksheet

	A	B	C	D	E
1	**Name**	**Surname**	**Invoice Number**	**Amount Incl VAT**	**Amount Excl VAT**
2	Billie	Moss	INV 1961045	202 347.06	177 497.42
3	Katharine	Lucas	INV 1072780	1 129 082.29	990 423.06
4	Lester	Rich	INV 1390667	369 630.67	324 237.43
5	Johnny	Carlton	INV 1985138	1 026 695.14	900 609.77
6	Ashley	Brady	INV 1593852	875 287.97	767 796.46
7	Lauren	Schultz	INV 1939541	1 440 353.78	1 263 468.23
8	Carolyn	Nichols	INV 1488644	380 303.93	333 599.94
9	Louis	Harvey	INV 1579705	439 607.48	385 620.60
10	Charlene	Stevenson	INV 1857410	157 204.90	137 899.04
11	Martin	Vick	INV 1429159	19 774.00	17 345.61
12	Jack	O'Donnell	INV 1264657	742 093.27	650 959.01
13	Vincent	Goldman	INV 1748388	509 176.04	446 645.65
14	Beth	McKenna	INV 1655859	307 180.58	269 456.65
15	Milton	Starr	INV 1602193	170 357.39	149 436.31
16	Tamara	Stone	INV 1236506	664 250.48	582 675.86
17	Mitchell	McClure	INV 1840703	1 043 261.77	915 141.90
18	Franklin	Watson	INV 1061427	664 908.75	583 253.29
19	Leroy	Monroe	INV 1340762	602 691.17	528 676.46
20	Glen	Abbott	INV 1488312	1 085 361.06	952 071.11
21	Judith	Singer	INV 1827348	244 642.12	214 598.35
22	Alice	Hall	INV 1013933	250 033.99	219 328.06
23	Bruce	Farrell	INV 1664415	11 201.67	9 826.03

Nesting Functions

In certain cases, you may need to use a function as one of the arguments of another function. For example, the following formula uses a nested AVERAGE function and compares the result with the value 50.

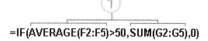

=IF(AVERAGE(F2:F5)>50,SUM(G2:G5),0)

The AVERAGE and SUM functions are nested within the IF function.

Valid returns

When a nested function is used as an argument, the nested function must return the same type of value that the argument uses. For example, if the argument returns a TRUE or FALSE value, the nested function must return a TRUE or FALSE value. If the function doesn't, Excel displays a #VALUE! error value.

> *A formula can contain up to **sixty-four (64)** levels of nested functions.*

Insert a Function within a Function

<u>**Method**</u>

1. From the **Formulas** tab, in the **Function Library** group, select the **Insert Function** button
2. Select the **first function** that you are going to be using e.g. **IF**
3. Select the argument into which you wish to insert the nested function
4. To **insert** the **nested function**, on the **left** of the **formula bar** click on the **drop-down** arrow to get a **list** of the most recently used functions

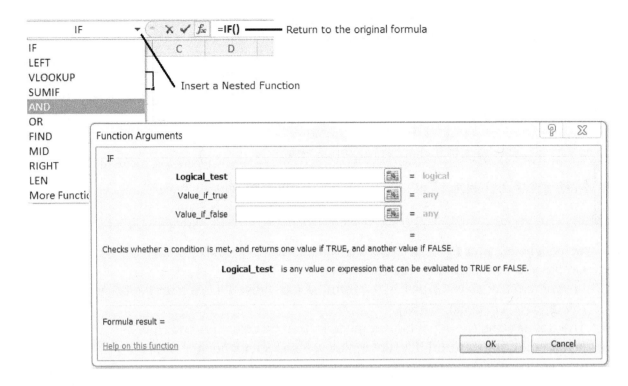

5. Either **select** the function you want to use or select **More Functions**
6. The **switch back** to your **original** formula, select it on the **Formula** bar

---

You can add a formula in one of three ways:

    1. **Type** *the formula, start with an equal (=) sign, Excel will guide you further*

    2. **Select** *the function you want from the* **Function Library** *on the* **Functions** *tab*

    3. *Click on the* **insert function** *button* f_x *next to the formula bar*

The last two methods will also provide you with a **dialog box** *to guide you through your formula.*

Absolute Referencing

Normally there is not a problem when you copy formulas. But you may get an error if you are referring to a **fixed cell**. If you do not fix your reference to cells in your formula, the reference will move relative to the new position you copy the formula to. If C1 contains a formula A1*B1 and you copy the formula to C2 the formula will **not** stay A1*B1, it will become A2*C2. If you now want all the formulas you copy to multiply by B1, you have to make that reference **absolute**.

So an **Absolute** reference is a fixed reference and a **Relative** reference is not.

Method

1. Select the cell where you want to enter the formula
2. Create your formula in the way you usually do
3. In your formula, as you type it in the **formula bar**, press **F4** just after the cell you want to fix (the reference will become **=$A$1**)
4. The **dollar** signs show that the reference is fixed on column A and Row 1
5. If you now **copy** or **AutoFill** your formula you should not get any errors

> *You can also add **Absolute** referencing afterwards by selecting in the **cell reference** inside the **formula bar** and then pressing **F4**. This functionality also works in formula dialog boxes. When you press **F4** it will fix different parts of the reference. The first press will be **both** row and column fix. If you press it more times you can choose to only fix on a row or a column or revert back to **relative referencing** (no **dollar** signs)*

Exercise: Absolute Referencing

Open file: **Absolute Referencing.xlsx**

Steps

- Select cell **B5** on the **Prices** sheet
- Enter the formula to get the amount exclusive of VAT
  =A5*(1/(1+B1))
- Use either the **Fill** handle or **Copy & Paste** to copy the formula up to cell **B12**
- You will observe that the results either do not make sense or contains an error
- Select cell **B5**
- Click on **B1** in the **formula bar** and press **F4**. The formula should read as follows now:
  =A5*(1/(1+$B$1))
- Use either the **Fill** handle or **Copy & Paste** to copy the formula up to cell **B12**
- The errors should now be corrected

Solution

	A	B
1	**VAT Rate**	14%
2		
3		
4	**Price (Incl. VAT)**	**Price (Excl VAT)**
5	270 000.00	236 842.11
6	56.23	49.32
7	99.99	87.71
8	89.65	78.64
9	5 000.00	4 385.96
10	480.00	421.05
11	224.00	196.49
12	114.00	100.00

Logical Functions

Logical functions return a TRUE or FALSE result. They are useful when testing the criteria of data. Based on that result you are able to do further analysis.

IF Function

The **IF** function returns one value if a condition you specify evaluates to TRUE, and another value if that condition evaluates to FALSE. For example, the formula **=IF(A1>10,"Over 10","10 or less")** returns "Over 10" if A1 is greater than 10, and "10 or less" if A1 is less than or equal to 10.

Syntax:	=IF(logical_test, [value_if_true], [value_if_false])
logical_test	Required. Any value or expression that can be evaluated to TRUE or FALSE. For example, A10=100 is a logical expression; if the value in cell A10 is equal to 100, the expression evaluates to TRUE. Otherwise, the expression evaluates to FALSE.
value_if_true	Optional. The value that you want to be returned if the **logical_test** argument evaluates to TRUE. For example, if the value of this argument is the text string "Within budget" and the **logical_test** argument evaluates to TRUE, the **IF** function returns the text "Within budget." If **logical_test** evaluates to TRUE and the **value_if_true** argument is omitted (that is, there is only a comma following the logical_test **argument**), the **IF** function returns **0** (zero). To display the word TRUE, use the logical value TRUE for the **value_if_true** argument.
value_if_false	Optional. The value that you want to be returned if the **logical_test** argument evaluates to FALSE. For example, if the value of this argument is the text string "Over budget" and the **logical_test** argument evaluates to FALSE, the **IF** function returns the text "Over budget." If **logical_test** evaluates to FALSE and the **value_if_false** argument is omitted, (that is, there is no comma following the **value_if_true** argument), the **IF** function returns the logical value FALSE. If **logical_test** evaluates to FALSE and the value of the **value_if_false** argument is blank (that is, there is only a comma following the **value_if_true** argument), the **IF** function returns the value 0 (zero).

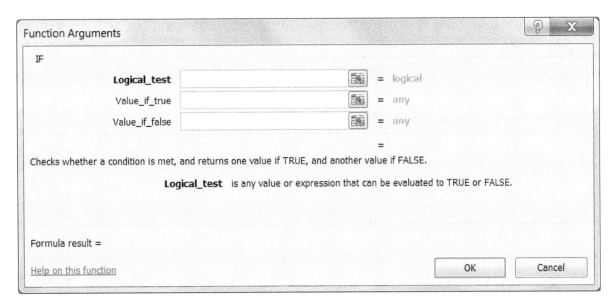

Method

1. Start the formula by typing an equal (=) sign in the cell followed by **IF** and an open bracket
   =IF(…
2. Excel will then prompt you to complete the variables. Optional Variables will be shown in square brackets

OR

1. On the **Formulas** tab, in the **Function Library** group, click **Logical**
2. **Select** the **IF** function
3. Complete the dialog box as shown above

OR

1. **Click** on the **Insert Function** button

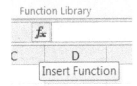

2. On the **Insert Function** dialog box, select the **Logical** category, then select the **IF** function from the list of functions

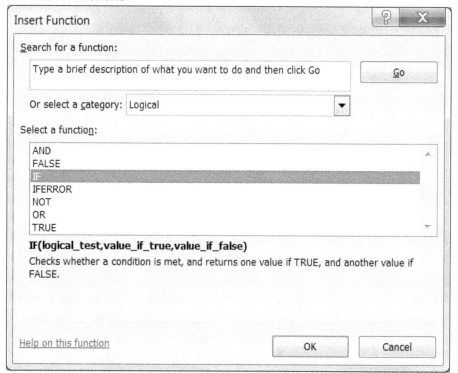

3. Click **OK**
4. Complete the **IF** dialog box as shown above

AND Function

Returns TRUE if all its arguments evaluate to TRUE; returns FALSE if one or more arguments evaluate to FALSE.

One common use for the **AND** function is to expand the usefulness of other functions that perform logical tests. For example, the **IF** function performs a logical test and then returns one value if the test evaluates to TRUE and another value if the test evaluates to FALSE. By using the **AND** function as the **logical_test** argument of the **IF** function, you can test many different conditions instead of just one.

Syntax:	=AND(logical1, [logical2], ...)
logical1	Required. The first condition that you want to test that can evaluate to either TRUE or FALSE.
logical2, ...	Optional. Additional conditions that you want to test that can evaluate to either TRUE or FALSE, up to a maximum of **255** conditions.

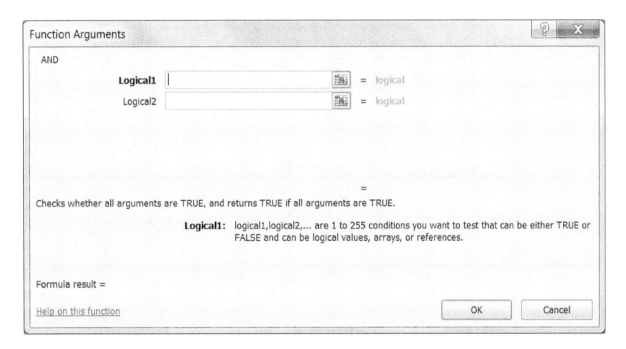

Method

1. Start the formula by typing an equal (=) sign in the cell followed by **AND** and an open bracket
   =AND(...
2. Excel will then prompt you to complete the variables. Optional Variables will be shown in square brackets

OR

1. On the **Formulas** tab, in the **Function Library** group, click **Logical**
2. **Select** the **AND** function
3. Complete the dialog box as shown above

OR

1. **Click** on the **Insert Function** button

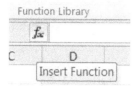

2. On the **Insert Function** dialog box, select the **Logical** category, then select the **AND** function from the list of functions

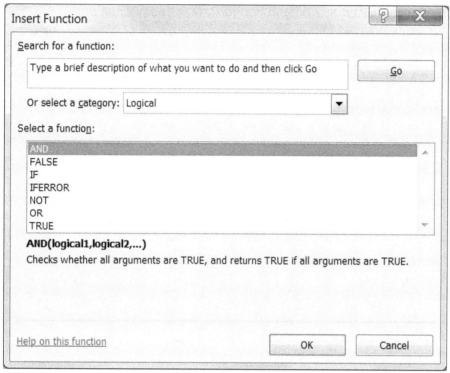

3. Click **OK**
4. Complete the **AND** dialog box as shown above

OR Function

Returns TRUE if any argument is TRUE; returns FALSE if all arguments are FALSE.

Syntax:	= OR(logical1, [logical2], ...)
logical1, logical2, ...	Logical1 is required, subsequent logical values are optional. 1 to 255 conditions you want to test that can be either TRUE or FALSE.

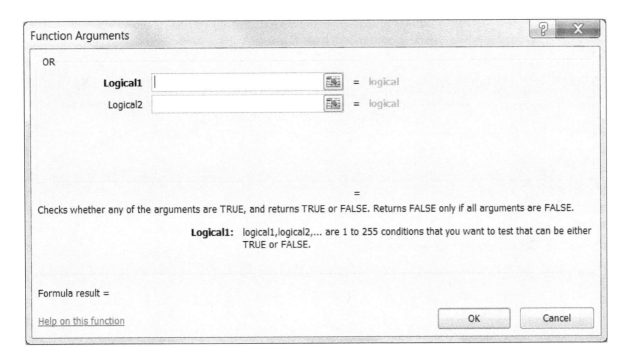

Method

1. Start the formula by typing an equal (=) sign in the cell followed by **OR** and an open bracket **=OR(...**
2. Excel will then prompt you to complete the variables. Optional Variables will be shown in square brackets

OR

1. On the **Formulas** tab, in the **Function Library** group, click **Logical**
2. **Select** the **OR** function
3. Complete the dialog box as shown above

OR

1. **Click** on the **Insert Function** button

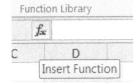

2. On the **Insert Function** dialog box, select the **Logical** category, then select the **OR** function from the list of functions

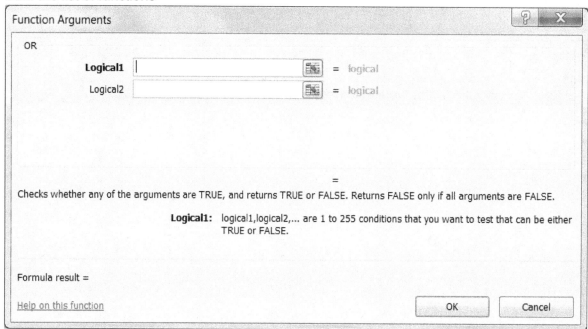

3. Click **OK**
4. Complete the **OR** dialog box as shown above

IFERROR Function

IFERROR returns a value you specify if a formula evaluates to an error; otherwise, returns the result of the formula. You would use the **IFERROR** function to trap and handle errors in a formula.

The following error types are evaluated: **#N/A**, **#VALUE!**, **#REF!**, **#DIV/0!**, **#NUM!**, **#NAME?**, or **#NULL!**.

Syntax:	= IFERROR(value, value_if_error)
value	Required. The argument that is checked for an error. In other words, your existing formula.
value_if_error	Required. The value to return if the formula evaluates to an error.

Method

1. **Select** a cell with an existing formula. For example: **=A2/B2**
2. Click on the **Formula bar** in the formula itself
3. Edit the formula by adding the **IFERROR** function:

   =IFERROR(A2/B2, "Error in calculation")

*Note: It is easier to first enter a formula and then to add the **IFERROR** function afterwards, otherwise you may not pick up if your original formula had an error.*

Exercise: Logical Functions

Open file: **Logical Functions.xlsx**

On the **AND** sheet

<u>Steps</u>

Get Sales by Department B in March

- Enter an **AND** function in cell **C2**. You can either type it in or use the **function libraries** and **dialog box**

logical1	A2="B"
logical2	MONTH(B2)=3

- The answer you get should be **TRUE** or **FALSE**
- Use either the **Fill** handle or **Copy & Paste** to copy the formula up to cell **C30**

Get Sales by Department A in May

- Enter an **AND** function in cell **D2**. You can either type it in or use the **function libraries** and dialog box

logical1	A2="A"
logical2	MONTH(B2)=5

- The answer you get should be **TRUE** or **FALSE**
- Use either the **Fill** handle or **Copy & Paste** to copy the formula up to cell **D30**

On the **OR** sheet

<u>Steps</u>

Valid board meetings should have either the CEO or the FD present

- Enter an **OR** function in cell **C2**. You can either type it in or use the **function libraries** and dialog box

logical1	B2="CEO"
logical2	B2="FD"

- The answer you get should be **TRUE** or **FALSE**

- Use either the **Fill** handle or **Copy & Paste** to copy the formula up to cell **C30**

On the **IF** sheet

<u>Steps</u>

Evaluate test scores and arrive at a result (Fail, Pass or Distinction)

- Enter an **IF** function in cell **B6**. You can either type it in or use the **function libraries** and dialog box

logical_test	A6<$C$1
value_if_true	$A$1
value_if_false	$A$2

You need to use absolute referencing here

- The answer you get should be **Pass** or **Fail**
- Use either the **Fill** handle or **Copy & Paste** to copy the formula up to cell **B16**

- Enter an **IF** function in cell **C6**. You can either type it in or use the **function libraries** and dialog box

logical_test	A6>$C$3
value_if_true	$A$3
value_if_false	"No Distinction"

You need to use absolute referencing here

- The answer you get should be **Distinction** or **No Distinction**
- Use either the **Fill** handle or **Copy & Paste** to copy the formula up to cell C16

Now combine the 2 formulas in D6

- Enter an **IF** function in cell **D6**. You can either type it in or use the **function libraries** and dialog box

logical_test	A6>$C$3
value_if_true	$A$3
value_if_false	"No Distinction"

You need to use absolute referencing here

- This is exactly as the formula in cell **C6**. So you could copy it from the formula bar in **C6**
- Now copy the formula in the cell **B6**. Copy **all** but the equal sign (**IF(A6<$C$1,$A$1,$A$2)**)
- In the cell **D6**, select the text **"No Distinction"** and **Paste** the above over it.
- The formula now reads as:

=IF(A6>$C$3,$A$3,IF(A6<$C$1,$A$1,$A$2))

- The answer you get should be **Fail**, **Pass** or **Distinction**
- Use either the **Fill** handle or **Copy & Paste** to copy the formula up to cell **D16**

On the **Data** sheet

Steps

- Select cell C2
- Click inside the formula bar and edit the formula to

=IFERROR(A2/B2,"")

- Either use the **Fill** functionality or copy and paste to copy the formula all the way to **C8**

Solution

AND worksheet

	A	B	C	D
1	Depratment	Date	Dept B in March	Dept A in May
2	A	26/02/2013	FALSE	FALSE
3	B	27/02/2013	FALSE	FALSE
4	A	28/02/2013	FALSE	FALSE
5	A	01/03/2013	FALSE	FALSE
6	B	02/03/2013	TRUE	FALSE
7	B	03/03/2013	TRUE	FALSE
8	B	04/03/2013	TRUE	FALSE
9	B	05/03/2013	TRUE	FALSE
10	B	06/03/2013	TRUE	FALSE

OR worksheet

	A	B	C
1	Meeting	Highest level Management	Valid board meeting (CEO or FD)
2	26/02/2013	CEO	TRUE
3	27/02/2013	FD	TRUE
4	28/02/2013	COO	FALSE
5	01/03/2013	FD	TRUE
6	02/03/2013	COO	FALSE
7	03/03/2013	MD	FALSE
8	04/03/2013	FD	TRUE
9	05/03/2013	Manger	FALSE
10	06/03/2013	MD	FALSE
11	07/03/2013	MD	FALSE
12	08/04/2013	CEO	TRUE
13	09/04/2013	Manger	FALSE

IF worksheet

	A	B	C	D
1	Fail	<	45%	
2	Pass			
3	Distinction	>	75%	
4				
5	Test Score	Pass/Fail	Distinction	Combined
6	10%	Fail	No Distinction	Fail
7	45%	Pass	No Distinction	Pass
8	44%	Fail	No Distinction	Fail
9	50%	Pass	No Distinction	Pass
10	65%	Pass	No Distinction	Pass
11	78%	Pass	Distinction	Distinction

Data worksheet

	A	B	C
1	Value 1	Value 2	Value 1 / Value 2
2	5	2	2.5
3	6	4	1.5
4	8	0	
5	9	12	0.75
6	0	3	0
7	3	4	0.75
8	12	A	

VLOOKUP Function

You can use the **VLOOKUP** function to search the first column of a range (range: Two or more cells on a sheet. The cells in a range can be adjacent or nonadjacent.) of cells, and then return a value from any cell on the same row of the range. For example, suppose that you have a list of employees contained in the range A2:C10. The employees' ID numbers are stored in the first column of the range, as shown in the following illustration.

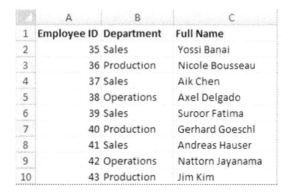

	A	B	C
1	Employee ID	Department	Full Name
2	35	Sales	Yossi Banai
3	36	Production	Nicole Bousseau
4	37	Sales	Aik Chen
5	38	Operations	Axel Delgado
6	39	Sales	Suroor Fatima
7	40	Production	Gerhard Goeschl
8	41	Sales	Andreas Hauser
9	42	Operations	Nattorn Jayanama
10	43	Production	Jim Kim

If you know the employee's ID number, you can use the **VLOOKUP** function to return either the department or the name of that employee. To obtain the name of employee number 38, you can use the formula **=VLOOKUP(38, A2:C10, 3, FALSE)**. This formula searches for the value 38 in the first column of the range A2:C10, and then returns the value that is contained in the third column of the range and on the same row as the lookup value ("Axel Delgado"). The V in **VLOOKUP** stands for vertical. Use **VLOOKUP** instead of **HLOOKUP** when your comparison values are located in a column to the left of the data that you want to find.

Syntax

VLOOKUP(lookup_value, table_array, col_index_num, [range_lookup])

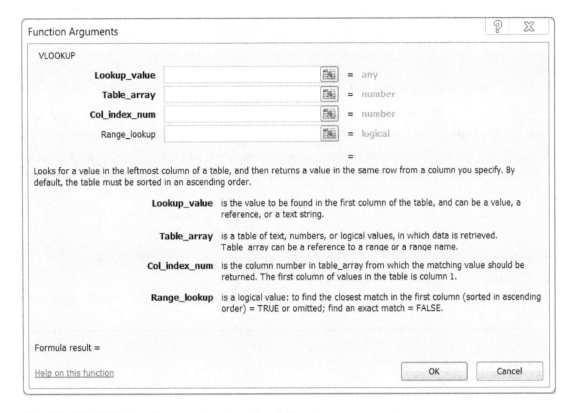

The **VLOOKUP** function syntax has the following arguments:

- *lookup_value* Required. The value to search in the first column of the table or range. The **lookup_value** argument can be a value or a reference. If the value you supply for the **lookup_value** argument is smaller than the smallest value in the first column of the **table_array** argument, **VLOOKUP** returns the #N/A error value.

- *table_array* Required. The range of cells that contains the data. You can use a reference to a range (for example, A2:D8), or a range name. The values in the first column of table_array are the values searched by **lookup_value**. These values can be text, numbers, or logical values. Uppercase and lowercase text are equivalent.

- *col_index_num* Required. The column number in the **table_array** argument from which the matching value must be returned. A **col_index_num** argument of 1 returns the value in the first column in table_array; a **col_index_num** of 2 returns the value in the second column in **table_array**, and so on.

- *range_lookup* Optional. A logical value that specifies whether you want **VLOOKUP** to find an exact match or an approximate match:

  - If **range_lookup** is either TRUE or is omitted, an exact or approximate match is returned. If an exact match is not found, the next largest value that is less than **lookup_value** is returned.

> If **range_lookup** is either TRUE or is omitted, the values in the first column of **table_array** must be placed in ascending sort order; otherwise, **VLOOKUP** might not return the correct value.
>
> If **range_lookup** is FALSE, the values in the first column of **table_array** do not need to be sorted.

  o   If the **range_lookup** argument is FALSE, **VLOOKUP** will find only an exact match. If there are two or more values in the first column of **table_array** that match the **lookup_value**, the first value found is used. If an exact match is not found, the error value #N/A is returned.

Method

1. Start the formula by typing an equal (**=**) sign in the cell followed by **VLOOKUP** and an open bracket **=VLOOKUP(...**
2. Excel will then prompt you to complete the variables. Optional Variables will be shown in square brackets

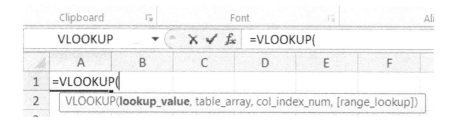

OR

1. On the **Formulas** tab, in the **Function Library** group, click **Lookup & Reference**
2. **Select** the **VLOOKUP** function
3. Complete the dialog box as shown above

OR

1. **Click** on the **Insert Function** button

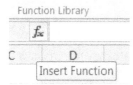

2. On the **Insert Function** dialog box, select the **Lookup & Reference** category, then select the **VLOOKUP** function from the list of functions

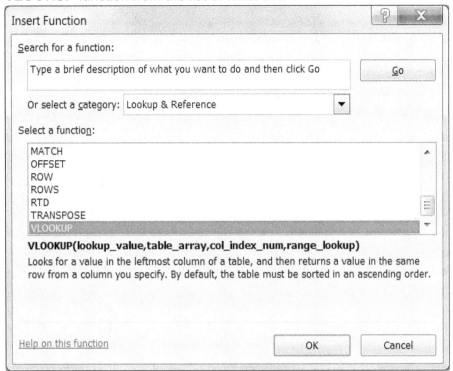

3. Click **OK**
4. Complete the **VLOOKUP** dialog box as shown above

Note: If **range_lookup** is FALSE and **lookup_value** is text, you can use the wildcard characters — the question mark (?) and asterisk (*) — in **lookup_value**. A question mark matches any single character; an asterisk matches any sequence of characters. If you want to find an actual question mark or asterisk, type a tilde (~) preceding the character.

Exercise: VLOOKUP Function

Open file: *VLOOKUP Function.xlsx*

Steps

- Select the **Page Views** worksheet
- Enter a **VLOOKUP** function in cell **B2**. You can either type it in or use the **function libraries** and dialog box

lookup_value	A2
table_array	Pages!A2:B39
col_index_num	2
range_lookup	0

- Fix the **table_array** reference (absolute reference) by using the **F4** key in either the **formula bar** or **VLOOKUP** dialog box

  Pages!$A$2:$B$39

- Use either the **Fill** handle or **Copy & Paste** to copy the formula up to cell **B14**

Alternative Steps using a Named Range

- **Delete** the formulas you added in the exercise above (**Page Views**, B2:B14)
- Select the data on the **Pages** worksheet (**A2:B39**)
- Click on [**Formulas**][**Defined Names**][**Define Name**]
- Set the name to **PageList**
- Click **OK**
- Enter a **VLOOKUP** function in cell **B2**. You can either type it in or use the **function libraries** and dialog box

lookup_value	A2
table_array	PageList
col_index_num	2
range_lookup	0

  (Remember you can see a list of **defined names** by pressing **F3** in the **formula bar** or **dialog box**)

- Use either the **Fill** handle or **Copy & Paste** to copy the formula up to cell **B14**

  (In the second alternative *you do not have to fix the data* as it refers to the **Named Range** created)

Named Ranges

Uses of Named Ranges:

- Instead of using a cell reference, use the named range in your formula
- Use the named range in your hyperlink
- Use the named range for navigating your worksheets

Naming rules:

- No Spaces
- No cell addresses
- Cannot begin with a number
- Maybe use underscore instead of space

A **name** is a meaningful shorthand that makes it easier to understand the purpose of a cell reference, constant, formula, or table, each of which may be difficult to comprehend at first glance. The following shows a common example of names and how they can improve clarity and understanding:

=SUM(C20:C30) can become

=SUM(FirstQuarterSales)

that is easier to read, maintain and protect.

Naming a Cell

Method

1. Select the cell you want to name
2. Select the **Name Box** and enter a **name**

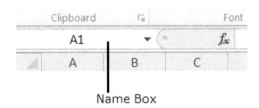

3. Press **Enter**

Using Column Headings to Name Columns

This is useful when you have a list and want the name the column heading to be the name of the Named Range.

Method

1. Select the **range** cell you want to name. Including the column labels
2. From the **Formulas** tab, in the **Defined Names** group, select **Create from Selection**

3. Select **Top row** (assuming your headings are in the top row)

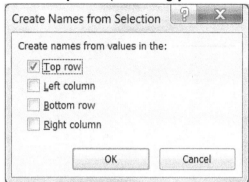

4. Select **OK**

Manually create a Name from a Selected Range

You can also first select a block of data and the manually create a name referring to it.

Method

1. Select the **range** cell you want to name. This can span multiple columns and rows
2. From the **Formulas** tab, in the **Defined Names** group, select **Define Name**
3. Complete the **New Name** dialog box

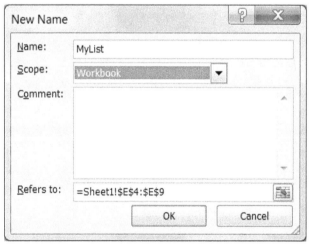

4. Select **OK**

Insert a Named Range in Formulas

Method

1. Create your **formula** the way you would normally
2. From the **Formulas** tab, in the **Defined Names** group, select **Use in Formula**
3. From the **list** of existing range names, select the name you want to insert

OR

1. Press **F3** to get a list of all **Named Ranges**

2. Select the **Named Range** and Select OK

Editing a Named Range

Method

1. From the **Formulas** tab, in the **Defined Names** group, select **Name Manager**
2. Select the **Named Range** you would like to edit
3. Select **Edit**

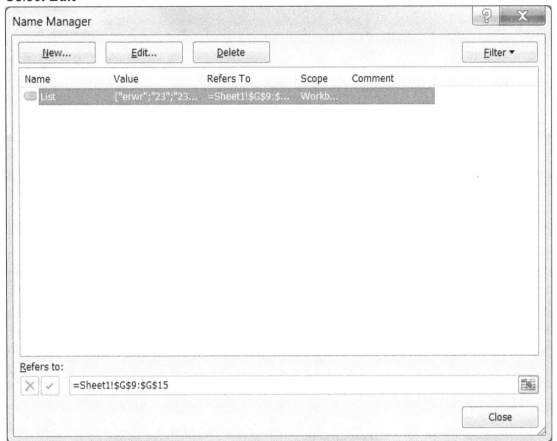

4. You can either change the **name** or change the **cell reference** in the **Refers to**

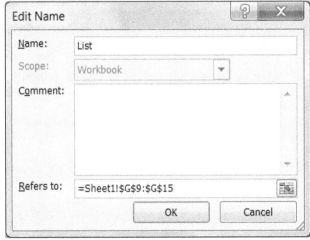

5. Select **OK**
6. Select **Close**

Navigating Named Ranges

Method

1. Select the drop-down arrow in the **Name Box**
2. Select the **Range Name** you want to navigate to

Exercise: Named Ranges

Open file: **Named Ranges.xlsx**

Steps

- Select cell **B1** on the **Prices** sheet
- Click in the **Name Box** (currently displaying **B1**) and enter **VATRate** as the new name
- Select cell **B5**
- Enter the formula to get the amount exclusive of VAT

    =A5*(1/(1+VATRate))

- Use either the **Fill** handle or **Copy & Paste** to copy the formula up to cell **B12**
- The results should now be correct without you having to use **Absolute Referencing**

- Select range (**A1:C6**) on the **Sales** worksheet
- Click on [**Formulas**][**Defined Names**][**Create from Selection**]
- Select **Top row**
- Click **OK**
- Select cell **F2**
- Enter the formula:

    =SUM(North)   - Remember to press **F3** when you need to enter **North**

- Select cell **F3**
- Enter the formula:

    =SUM(East)   - Remember to press **F3** when you need to enter **East**

- Select cell **F4**
- Enter the formula:

    =SUM(West)   - Remember to press **F3** when you need to enter **West**

Solution

Prices worksheet

	A	B
1	**VAT Rate**	14%
2		
3		
4	**Price (Incl. VAT)**	**Price (Excl VAT)**
5	270 000.00	236 842.11
6	56.23	49.32
7	99.99	87.71
8	89.65	78.64
9	5 000.00	4 385.96
10	480.00	421.05
11	224.00	196.49
12	114.00	100.00

Sales worksheet

	A	B	C	D	E	F
1	**North**	**East**	**West**			
2	500	956	80		**North Sales**	2 687
3	600	598	695		**East Sales**	12 976
4	598	4 988	958		**West Sales**	3 057
5	635	885	468			
6	354	5 549	856			

Mathematical Functions

SUMIF Function

You use the **SUMIF** function to sum the values in a range that meet criteria that you specify. For example, suppose that in a column that contains numbers, you want to sum only the values that are larger than 5. You can use the following formula:

 =SUMIF(B2:B25,">5")

In this example, the criteria are applied the same values that are being summed. If you want, you can apply the criteria to one range and sum the corresponding values in a different range. For example, the formula **=SUMIF(B2:B5, "John", C2:C5)** sums only the values in the range **C2:C5**, where the corresponding cells in the range **B2:B5** equal **"John"**.

Syntax:	=SUMIF(range, criteria, [sum_range])
range	Required. The range of cells that you want to be evaluated by criteria. Cells in each range must be numbers or names, arrays, or references that contain numbers. Blank and text values are ignored.
criteria	Required. The criteria in the form of a number, expression, a cell reference, text, or a function that defines which cells will be added. For example, criteria can be expressed as **32**, **">32"**, **B5**, **"32"**, **"apples"**, or **TODAY()**. ***Important*** Any text criteria or any criteria that include logical or mathematical symbols must be enclosed in double quotation marks ("). If the criteria are numeric, double quotation marks are not required.
sum_range	Optional. The actual cells to add if you want to add cells other than those specified in the **range** argument. If the **sum_range** argument is omitted, Excel adds the cells that are specified in the **range** argument (the same cells to which the criteria is applied).

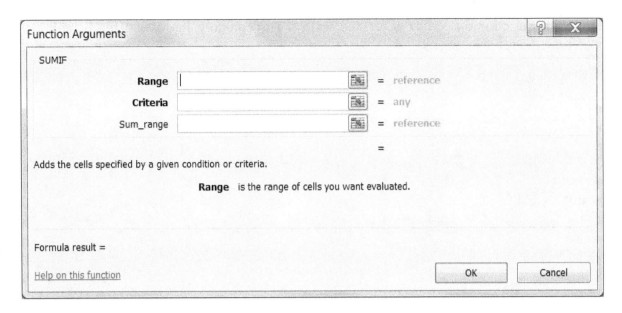

Method

1. Start the formula by typing an equal (=) sign in the cell followed by **SUMIF** and an open bracket **=SUMIF(...**
2. Excel will then prompt you to complete the variables. Optional Variables will be shown in square brackets

OR

1. On the **Formulas** tab, in the **Function Library** group, click **Math & Trig**
2. **Select** the **SUMIF** function
3. Complete the dialog box as shown above

OR

1. **Click** on the **Insert Function** button

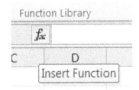

2. On the **Insert Function** dialog box, select the **Math & Trig** category, then select the **SUMIF** function from the list of functions

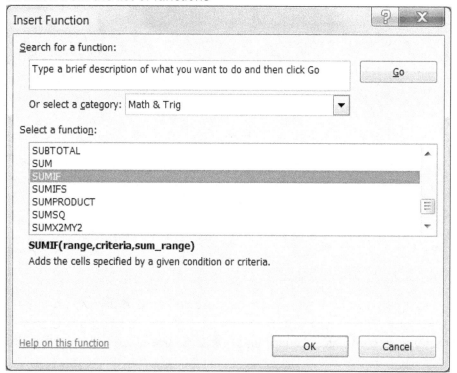

3. Click **OK**
4. Complete the **SUMIF** dialog box as shown above

AVERAGEIF Function

Returns the average (arithmetic mean) of all the cells in a range that meet a given criteria.

Syntax:	=AVERAGEIF(range, criteria, [average_range])
range	Required. One or more cells to average, including numbers or names, arrays, or references that contain numbers.
criteria	Required. The criteria in the form of a number, expression, cell reference, or text that defines which cells are averaged. For example, criteria can be expressed as **32**, **"32"**, **">32"**, **"apples"**, or **B4**. *Important* Any text criteria or any criteria that include logical or mathematical symbols must be enclosed in double quotation marks ("). If the criteria are numeric, double quotation marks are not required.
average_range	Optional. The actual set of cells to average. If omitted, the **range** is used.

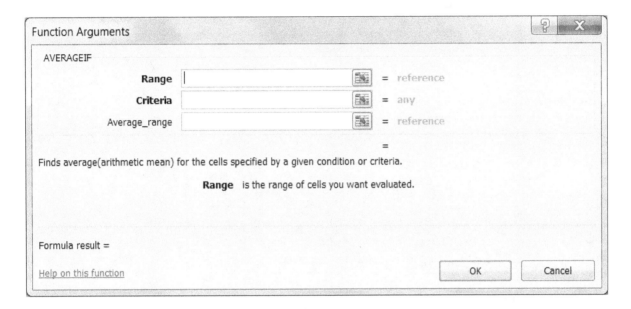

Method

1. Start the formula by typing an equal (=) sign in the cell followed by **AVERAGEIF** and an open bracket **=AVERAGEIF(...**
2. Excel will then prompt you to complete the variables. Optional Variables will be shown in square brackets

OR

1. On the **Formulas** tab, in the **Function Library** group, click **More Functions, Statistical**
2. **Select** the **AVERAGEIF** function
3. Complete the dialog box as shown above

OR

1. **Click** on the **Insert Function** button

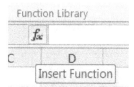

2. On the **Insert Function** dialog box, select the **Statistical** category, then select the **AVERAGEIF** function from the list of functions

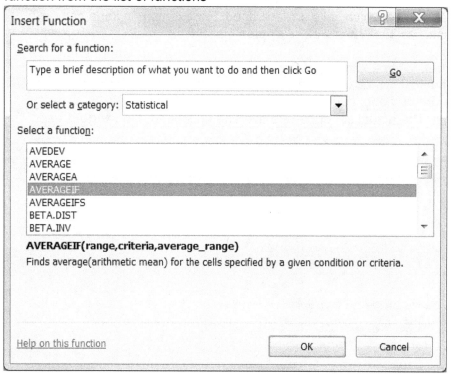

3. Click **OK**
4. Complete the **AVERAGEIF** dialog box as shown above

Exercise: SUMIF Function

Open file: **SUMIF Function.xlsx**

Steps

- Enter a **SUMIF** function in cell **F3**, you can either type it in or use the **function libraries** and dialog box

range	$C$2:$C$28
criteria	E3
sum_range	$B$2:$B$28

Fix the **range** and **sum_range** reference (absolute reference) by using the **F4** key in either the **formula bar** or SUMIF dialog box

- Use either the **Fill** handle or **Copy & Paste** to copy the formula up to cell **F5**
- The totals for the **Summary** should be the same as the **asset list**

Solution

	A	B	C	D	E	F
1	**Asset Number**	**Cost Price**	**Classification**			
2	A# 26598	331 924	Motor Vehicles		Summary	
3	A# 26599	253 039	Furniture		Land and Buildings	2 442 891
4	A# 26600	18 624	Furniture		Motor Vehicles	2 308 592
5	A# 26601	338 795	Motor Vehicles		Furniture	2 041 701
6	A# 26602	168 896	Furniture			6 793 184
7	A# 26603	180 466	Furniture			

Conditional Formatting

Use a conditional format to help you visually explore and analyse data, detect critical issues, and identify patterns and trends. Conditional formatting helps you visually answer specific questions about your data. You can apply conditional formatting to a cell range, a Microsoft Excel table, or a PivotTable report.

The benefits of conditional formatting

Whenever you analyse data, you often ask yourself questions, such as:

- Where are the exceptions in a summary of profits over the past five years?
- What are the trends in a marketing opinion poll over the past two years?
- Who has sold more than 50,000 this month?
- What is the overall age distribution of employees?
- Which products have greater than 10% revenue increases from year to year?
- Who are the highest performing and lowest performing students in the class?

Conditional formatting helps to answer these questions by making it easy to highlight interesting cells or ranges of cells, emphasize unusual values, and visualize data by using data bars, colour scales, and icon sets. A conditional format changes the appearance of a cell range based on conditions (or criteria). If the condition is true, the cell range is formatted based on that condition; if the conditional is false, the cell range is not formatted based on that condition.

Add Conditional Formatting

Method

1. Select the **cells** for which you want to add conditional formatting
2. From the **Home** tab, in the **Styles** group, select **Conditional Formatting**
3. Select the rule you want to apply from the list
4. Each rule is further divided into sub types, for example, **Highlight Cells Rules**

5. Select the sub type, for example, **Greater Than…**

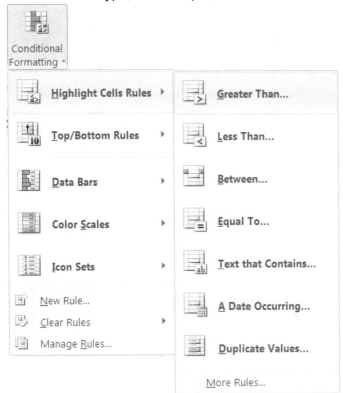

6. Enter the **criteria**, remember to complete the format requirements in the **with** box

7. Select **OK**

Add Conditional Formatting across Rows

Method

1. Select the **entire** range that you would like to apply the conditional formatting to
2. From the **Home** tab, in the **Styles** group, select **Conditional Formatting**
3. Select **New Rule** from the list
4. In **Select a Rule Type**, **select Use a formula to determine which cells to format**
5. Enter your criteria ensuring you **fix** the **column** reference as below:

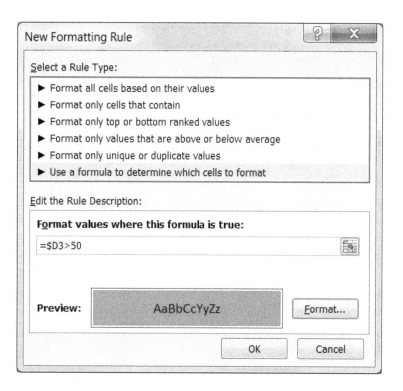

6. Select the **Format...** button
7. Set the format parameters and select **OK**, **OK**

To ensure you apply the Conditional Formatting to the entire row:

> **Highlight** *the entire table of data*

> *Select **Use a Formula to determine which cells to format***

> *Fix your column reference e.g.* **=$C**

By doing this you will ensure that when the formula is applied to the other cells, it will continue to refer to the specified column $c, else it will only highlight the first column of data.

Copy Conditional Formatting

Method

1. Select the cells that have the **conditional formatting** you want to **copy**
2. From the **Home** tab, select the **Format Painter**

   ◇ Format Painter

3. Select the **cells** you want to **format**
4. Press **ESC** when you finished

OR

1. Select the **cells** that have the **conditional formatting** you want to **copy**
2. Select **copy**
3. **Highlight** the **destination** cells
4. **Right** click and select **Paste Special**, **Formats**, **OK**

Change Conditional Formatting

Method

1. From the **Home** tab, in the **Styles** group, select **Conditional Formatting**
2. Select **Manage Rules**
3. From the **Conditional Formatting Rules Manager** dialog box, select the rule you wish to change
4. Select the **Edit Rule** box
5. Make the required changes
6. Select **OK**, **OK**

Remove Conditional Formatting

Method

1. From the **Home** tab, in the **Styles** group, select **Conditional Formatting**
2. Select **Manage Rules**
3. Select the rule you want to remove
4. Select the **Delete Rule** button
5. Select **OK**

Highlight Duplicates

Method

1. From the **Home** tab, in the **Styles** group, select **Conditional Formatting**
2. Select **Highlight Cell Rules**
3. Select **Duplicate Values**
4. Complete the formatting requirements in the **Duplicate Values** dialog box
5. Select **OK**

Exercise: Conditional Formatting

Open file: *Conditional Formatting.xlsx*

Steps

- Select the cells **B2:B21** on **Sheet1**
- Click on [**Home**][**Styles**][**Conditional Formatting**][**Highlight Cells Rules**][**Duplicate Values...**]
- Click **OK**
- You should now see the values that have duplicates

	A	B
1	#	Ref #
2	1	10253
3	2	10254
4	3	10255
5	4	10256
6	5	10257
7	6	10258
8	7	10259
9	8	10260
10	9	10261
11	10	10262
12	11	10263
13	12	10264
14	13	10265
15	14	10266
16	15	10267
17	16	10256
18	17	10269
19	18	10270
20	19	10271
21	20	10272

- Select the cells **C2:C21** on **Sheet1**
- Click on **[Home][Styles][Conditional Formatting][Highlight Cells Rules][Greater Than…]**
- Enter **120 000** in the **value** box and select **Green Fill with Dark Green Text**

- Click **OK**
- You should now see the values **greater** than **120 000**

	A	B	C
1	#	Ref #	Amount
2	1	10253	142 050
3	2	10254	107 572
4	3	10255	32 074
5	4	10256	156 578
6	5	10257	53 671
7	6	10258	12 982
8	7	10259	101 165
9	8	10260	82 713
10	9	10261	123 058
11	10	10262	67 732
12	11	10263	51 894
13	12	10264	33 650
14	13	10265	89 740
15	14	10266	98 345
16	15	10267	88 929
17	16	10256	95 641
18	17	10269	176 305
19	18	10270	37 896
20	19	10271	45 910
21	20	10272	143 313

Auditing a Formula

The Formula Auditing group options can help to check worksheets to ensure the formulas are consistent and have no errors.

It is also useful when checking for accuracy or finding the source of an error can be difficult when the formula uses precedent or dependent cells:

- **Precedent** cells are cells that are referred to by a formula in another cell e.g. if cell **D10** contains the formula **=B5**, cell **B5** is a precedent to cell **D10**.

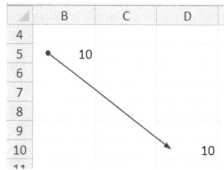

- **Dependent** cells are cells that contain formulas that refer to other cells e.g. if cell **D10** contains the formula **=B5**, cell **D10** is a dependent of cell **B5**.

Trace Precedent/Dependent Arrows

Method

1. From the **Formulas** tab, in the **Formula Auditing** group, select **Trace Precedents** or **Trace Dependents**
2. All cells **leading up to** or **being used** in the formula will be displayed

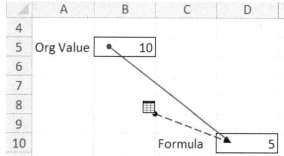

3. If the below icon is shown, it means that cells from **another worksheet** are being referenced

4. To navigate to that particular **worksheet**, **double** click the **dotted** line
5. The **Go To** dialog box will be displayed
6. Select the **Reference**, select **OK**

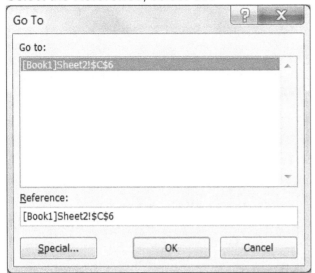

7. You will be navigated to the worksheet with the cell references

Remove Arrows

Method

1. From the **Formulas** tab, in the **Formula Auditing** group, select **Remove Arrows**

OR

1. Select the **drop-down** arrow, select **Remove Precedent Arrows** or **Remove Dependent Arrows**

Exercise: Auditing a Formula

Open file: *Auditing a Formula.xlsx*

Steps

- Select cell **F8** on **Sheet1**
- Click on [**Formulas**][**Formula Auditing**][**Trace Precedents**]

	A	B	C	D	E	F
1						
2			VAT Rate	14%		
3						
4		#	Date	Sales (Excl VAT)	Commission	VAT
5		1	01/01/2012	69 209.00	1 730.23	9 689.26
6		2	01/02/2012	57 515.00	1 437.88	8 052.10
7		3	01/03/2012	54 998.00	1 374.95	7 699.72
8		4	01/04/2012	62 282.00	1 557.05	8 719.48

- The arrows will show which variables are used to calculate the value of cell **F8**
- Click on [**Formulas**][**Formula Auditing**][**Remove Arrows**]

- Select cell **D2** on **Sheet1**
- Click on [**Formulas**][**Formula Auditing**][**Trace Dependents**]

▲	A	B	C	D	E	F
1						
2			VAT Rate	14%		
3						
4		#	Date	Sales (Excl VAT)	Commission	VAT
5		1	01/01/2012	69 209.00	1 730.23	9 689.26
6		2	01/02/2012	57 515.00	1 437.88	8 052.10
7		3	01/03/2012	54 998.00	1 374.95	7 699.72
8		4	01/04/2012	62 282.00	1 557.05	8 719.48
9		5	01/05/2012	66 954.00	1 673.85	9 373.56
10		6	01/06/2012	60 649.00	1 516.23	8 490.86
11		7	01/07/2012	63 148.00	1 578.70	8 840.72
12		8	01/08/2012	72 409.00	1 810.23	10 137.26
13		9	01/09/2012	58 004.00	1 450.10	8 120.56
14		10	01/10/2012	71 498.00	1 787.45	10 009.72
15		11	01/11/2012	65 965.00	1 649.13	9 235.10
16		12	01/12/2012	59 985.00	1 499.63	8 397.90
17		13	01/01/2013	70 403.00	1 760.08	9 856.42
18		14	01/02/2013	73 417.00	1 835.43	10 278.38
19		15	01/03/2013	73 898.00	1 847.45	10 345.72

- The arrows will show where cell **D2** is used in a formula
- Click on [**Formulas**][**Formula Auditing**][**Remove Arrows**]
- Select cell **E5** on **Sheet1**
- Click on [**Formulas**][**Formula Auditing**][**Trace Precedents**]

- The arrows will show which variables are used to calculate the value of cell **E5**
- **Double click** the **dotted line**

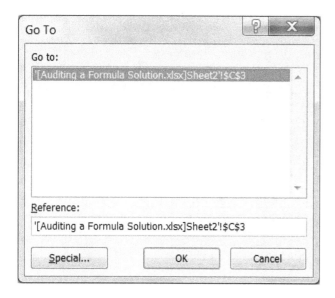

- Select the reference in the **Go To** dialog box:
- Click **OK**
- You will now be navigated to the cell on **Sheet2**

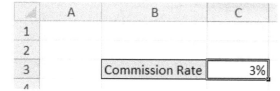

PivotTables

A PivotTable is useful to summarize, analyse, explore, and present summary data. A PivotChart can help you visualize PivotTable summary data so that you can easily see comparisons, patterns, and trends. Both enable you to make informed decisions about critical data in your enterprise.

A PivotTable is an interactive way to quickly summarise large amounts of data. Use a PivotTable to analyse numerical data in detail and to answer unanticipated questions about your data. A PivotTable is specially designed for:

- Querying large amounts of data in many user-friendly ways.
- Subtotaling and aggregating numeric data, summarising data by categories and subcategories, and creating custom calculations and formulas.
- Expanding and collapsing levels of data to focus your results and drilling down to details from the summary data for areas of interest to you.
- Moving rows to columns or columns to rows (or "pivoting") to see different summaries of the source data.
- Filtering, sorting, grouping, and conditionally formatting the most useful and interesting subset of data to enable you to focus on the information that you want.

Original Worksheet

	A	B	C	D	E	F	G
1	Number	Name	Surname	Invoice Number	Amount Incl VAT	Amount Excl VAT	Date
2	1	Kristina	Chung	INV 1614589	476 144.56	417 670.67	24/02/2012
3	2	Paige	Chen	INV 1253236	1 084 906.46	951 672.33	23/02/2012
4	3	Sherri	Melton	INV 1095721	113 729.51	99 762.73	22/02/2012
5	4	Gretchen	Hill	INV 1974050	99 620.19	87 386.13	21/02/2012
6	5	Karen	Puckett	INV 1670358	952 765.64	835 759.33	20/02/2012
7	6	Patrick	Song	INV 1681825	1 243 839.80	1 091 087.54	19/02/2012
8	7	Elsie	Hamilton	INV 1735227	332 175.22	291 381.77	18/02/2012
9	8	Hazel	Bender	INV 1287222	1 382 707.99	1 212 901.75	17/02/2012
10	9	Malcolm	Wagner	INV 1819631	285 682.37	250 598.57	16/02/2012
11	10	Dolores	McLaughlin	INV 1494106	1 215 392.81	1 066 134.04	15/02/2012
12	11	Francis	McNamara	INV 1510058	1 316 091.40	1 154 466.14	14/02/2012
13	12	Sandy	Raynor	INV 1146637	1 237 335.68	1 085 382.18	13/02/2012
14	13	Marion	Moon	INV 1437476	1 022 170.58	896 640.86	12/02/2012
15	14	Beth	Woodard	INV 1328954	177 916.86	156 067.42	11/02/2012
16	15	Julia	Desai	INV 1871155	1 382 595.33	1 212 802.92	10/02/2012
17	16	Jerome	Wallace	INV 1151416	838 396.72	735 435.72	09/02/2012

PivotTable

Date	(Multiple Items)
Row Labels	**Amount Excl VAT**
Becky	899 387.49
Clyde	760 722.83
Erin	450 367.17
Norma	1 079 607.54
Paul	46 364.46
Ray	537 746.32
Rebecca	1 152 349.95
Ron	833 769.30
Tonya	1 226 024.68
Tracey	582 437.58
Grand Total	**7 568 777.32**

PivotChart

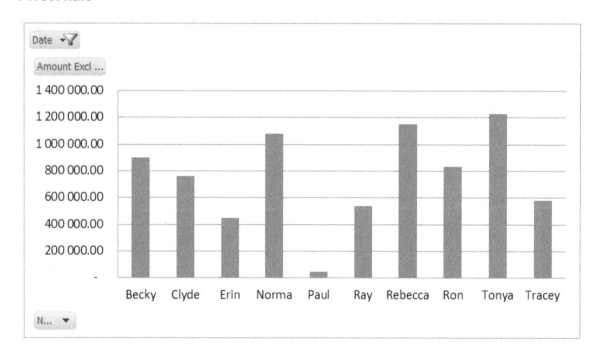

Concept and Layout

An important point to remember when working with PivotTables is that you are working in a layout slightly different to a normal Excel worksheet. A PivotTable has its own Ribbon and that alone provides functionality specific to the PivotTable.

Although one can format a cell using the format tools on the Home tab of the Ribbon, a PivotTable provides its own format cells option on its Ribbon as it is treated as a separate entity.

A PivotTable has its own layout and is split up into 4 sections.

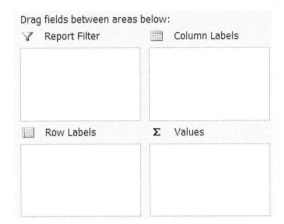

Each of the above sections is used to show fields from the PivotTable source data, each sections having its own purpose.

Report Filter	This section assists in providing a **third dimension** to your data. It can also provide a more **summarised/filtered** view of the rest of the fields displayed in other sections. When placing a field in this section it **reduces** the number of items within a PivotTable and in some instances prevents the PivotTable number of items limitation from being reached. If you **include** a **Report Filter** field in your PivotTable you can choose to display the PivotTable pages on **separate worksheets**. Select the **Options** tab under the **PivotTable** sub-group, select the drop-down arrow next to the **Options** button on the **PivotTable** group and from here select **Show Report Filter Pages…**. Excel will automatically replicate each page's data on a separate worksheet.
Column Labels	You would place **fields** in this section when you want to **group** the data by specific field e.g. by customer. Your customers will appear in the **columns going across**.
Row Labels	You would place **fields** in this section when wanting to **group** the data by a specific field. E.g. by Customer. Your customers will appear in the **rows going down**.
Values	You would normally place **fields** in this section where their **values** are numbers such as a **quantity** or **amount** field e.g. **Customer Sales**. Calculations such as **sum**, **average**, **min**, **max** etc. can be used in these fields. This section has to contain at least one field.

PivotTable Field List

The PivotTable Field List contains the fields available for your **PivotTable**, based on the fields in the range that the PivotTable is based on. In addition, there are areas where you can add Report filters, sections that list the row and column fields and a section for the values.

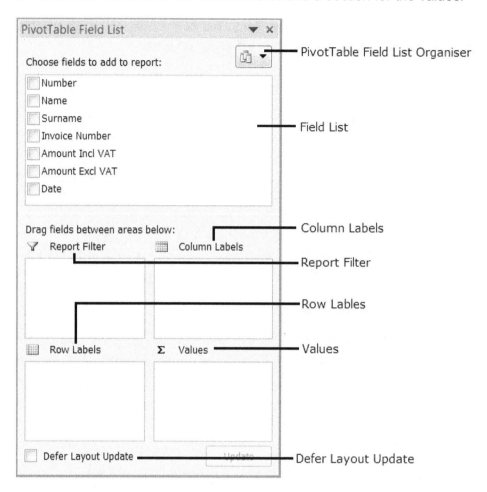

Turn the Field List On/Off

The **PivotTable Field List** is only visible while you are within the PivotTable. If you are within the PivotTable and it is still not visible, **right click** and select **Show Field List**. You can also turn the field list on and off from the Ribbon.

Method

1. Select any cell in the **PivotTable**
2. From the **Options** tab, in the **Show** group, select **Field List**

OR

1. Select any cell in the **PivotTable**
2. **Right** click and select **Show/Hide Field List**

*PivotTables are updated each time a **field** is **added**, **removed** or **moved** to a different position. For PivotTables based on large data sets, these actions can take some time to complete. If you would rather manually update, select **Defer Layout Update**.*

PivotTable Ribbon

The PivotTable is generated from the **Insert** tab on the **Ribbon**. From the PivotTable icon, you can select PivotTable or PivotChart.

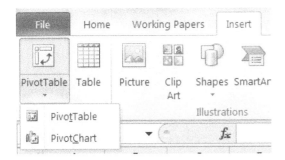

Once the PivotTable has been inserted, a **PivotTable Tools Ribbon** becomes available. The new Ribbon has 2 tabs, the **Options** tab and the **Design** tab.

PivotTable Layout

You can change the general settings of the PivotTable layout. This layout will determine how the PivotTable will function and look. The different layouts are listed below.

Compact Form	By **default**, Excel puts your PivotTable in this format. It is used to keep related data from spreading horizontally off the screen and to help minimise scrolling. Beginning fields on the side are contained in one column and are indented to show the nested column relationship.
Outline Form	Used to outline the data in the classic PivotTable style.
Tabular Form	Used to see all data in a traditional table format and to easily copy cells to another worksheet.

Method

1. From the Design tab, in the Layout group select Report Layout

2. Select the needed Layout

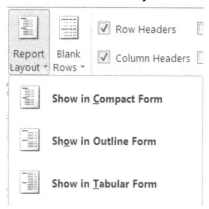

Create a PivotTable

To create a PivotTable, you need to identify these two elements in your data:

- Have a list in Excel with data fields (headings) and rows of related data
- Identify which fields are going into your design

> *When selecting your data range and you know that the rows of the list will **grow**, ensure that you select **extra rows** with your selection.*
>
> *Click on column **A** and **drag** to the **last column** of the list. This will ensure you select the range down to the last row in Excel.*
>
> *Also if your data has **blank rows**, you can still use it but you have to **manually** select all the data you want to use.*

Method

1. Select any **cell** in the **data** list
2. From the **Insert** tab, in the **Tables** group, select **PivotTable**

PivotTable

3. Make sure that **Select a table or range** is selected

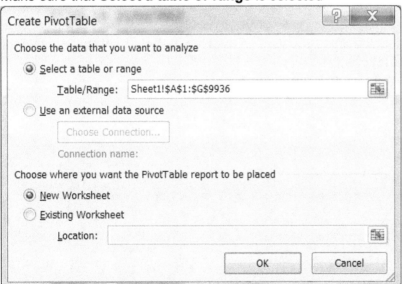

4. Make sure your data is listed in the **Table/Range** box
5. Select where you want the PivotTable to go, either in the **Existing Worksheet** or **New Worksheet**
6. Select **OK**

7. A **blank** PivotTable will now be displayed

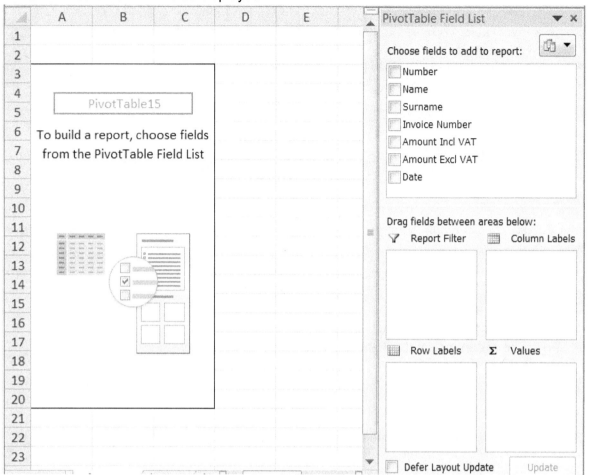

8. In the **Field List** either select the fields you want in the **Row Labels** or drag them into the **Row Labels** area on the **Field List** box
9. Repeat for **Report Filter**, **Column Labels** and **Values**

Format a PivotTable

PivotTable Styles

Now that you have the PivotTable designed, as you need it, you may want to format it to look more professional. Excel provides a gallery of styles ready for you to use. You can also add or remove banding of rows and columns.

Method

1. Select any **cell** in the **PivotTable** report
2. From the **Design** tab in the **PivotTable** Styles group, select one of the visible styles or scroll through all the available styles

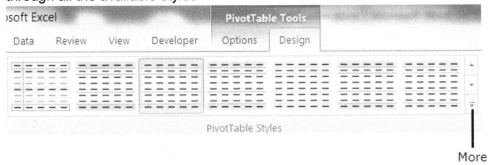

3. You can also click on the **more** button to see all the styles available. Or you can create your own style by clicking on **New Pivot Style…** at the bottom of the list
4. To remove a format, select **Clear** at the bottom of the list

PivotTable Style Options

Another way to format your PivotTable is to use the Style Options. Style Options can get applied to a PivotTable that has had a Style applied or not. You can add or remove banding (alternating a darker and lighter background) of rows and columns. Banding makes it easier to read and scan data.

Method

1. Select any **cell** in the **PivotTable**
2. From the **Design** tab, in the **PivotTable Style Options** group, select the type of banding required for either rows, columns or row or column headers

Remove/Add and Move Fields

When selecting a field from the data area to move or remove, you need to select the field by placing the mouse pointer on the border of the field and clicking when the pointer changes to a normal arrow pointer.

Fields that appear in the PivotTable will have a tick in their check box on the Field List. Deselecting this check box will remove the field from the PivotTable.

Remove a Field

Method

1. From the Field List select the check box next to the field you wish to remove

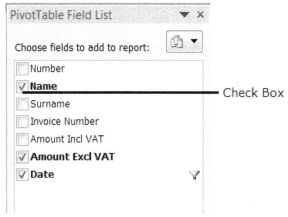

OR

1. From the Field List, select the drop-down arrow next to the field
2. Select **Remove Field**

Add a Field

Method

1. Select the check box next to the field in the **Field List**

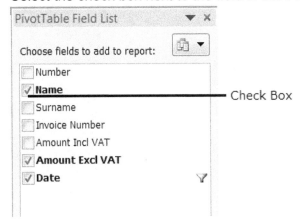
Check Box

OR

1. Select the **Field** in the **Field List** and drag it to the desired area e.g. Report Filter

Move Fields within the Table

Method

1. From the Field List, drag the field to the desired area

OR

1. From the **Field List**, select the **drop-down** arrow next to the field
2. Select **Move Up**, **Move Down**, etc.

Changes to Source Data

Once a PivotTable Report has been created, it can easily be updated if the data in the original worksheet (source data) changes.

Method

1. Select any cell in the **PivotTable**
2. From the **Options** tab, in the **Data** group, select **Refresh**

Refresh

3. The table is now updated with the changes made to the **source** data

OR

1. **Right** click the **PivotTable**
2. Select **Refresh**

Filter a PivotTable Report

You can set the data that will be displayed in your PivotTable, based on the selections you set. You use the drop-down arrows next to the headings to do this. Note that the icons change if you have filtered on a Field.

Method

1. Select the drop-down arrow in a field you wish to filter

2. Select the check boxes of the items you would like displayed

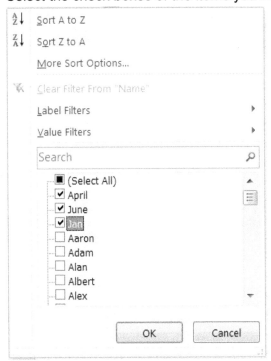

3. Select **OK**
4. To display all the items, select **Select All**

*You can **control** whether the filter button is available by setting or clearing the **Display field caption and filter drop-downs** check box in the **Display** tab of the PivotTable **Option** dialog box, or by clicking **Field Headers** in the **Show** group on the **Options** tab.*

*You **cannot** filter by **colour**, **font colour**, or **icon** set in a PivotTable report or PivotChart report.*

If you select the Select All check box, it will either select all items or de-select all items.

Field Settings in Row/Column Labels

Once you have created your PivotTable with the necessary fields, you may want to adjust certain field settings.

Turn off Subtotals or Change Calculation

Method

1. Select the desired **field**
2. From the **Options** tab, in the **Active Field** group, select **Field Settings**

OR

1. **Right Click** on the field and select **Field Settings**
2. Select the **Subtotals & Filters** tab

3. Select **None** to turn **off** subtotals for that particular field
4. Select **Custom** to change the method of **calculation**, and select the desired function e.g. Average
5. Select **OK**

---

*A quick way to turn **off all** subtotals:*

> *From the **Design** tab, in the **Layout** group, select **Subtotals***

> *Select **Do Not Show Subtotals***

Create a Custom Name

You are able to adjust the field names in the PivotTable. If you change the name of the field in the PivotTable, it will not affect the name in your source data.

In the Values area, you may find that the PivotTable will automatically put in Sum of, in front of the fields name.

Method

1. Select the desired **field**
2. From the **Options** tab, in the **Active Field** group, select **Field Settings**

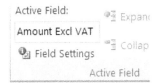

OR

1. Select the desired **field**
2. **Right** click on the field and select **Field Settings**
3. Select the **Custom Name** box

4. Enter a new name
5. Select **OK**

OR

1. Select the cell that contains the field
2. **Enter** the new field name
3. Press **Enter**

A **Custom Name** has to be **unique**. If you already have a field with a name you wish to use again (in the source data), then you can make it unique by adding a **space** after the name.

Value Field Settings in Values

Cells within a Pivot Table can be formatted as you normally would, use the Value Field Settings dialog box. Besides this option, within a PivotTable, you can use the Number Format button on the Field Settings dialog box to change the number format. This will only display the number tab of the Format Cells dialog box so it cannot be used to change the font alignment etc.

Change Number Format

Method

1. Select the desired field
2. From the **Options** tab, in the **Active Field** group, select **Field Settings**

OR

1. Select the desired **field**
2. **Right** click on the field and select **Field Settings**
3. Select **Number Format**

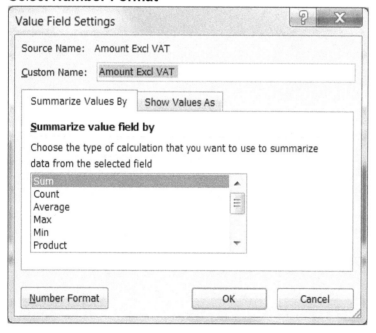

4. Select the desired **format**

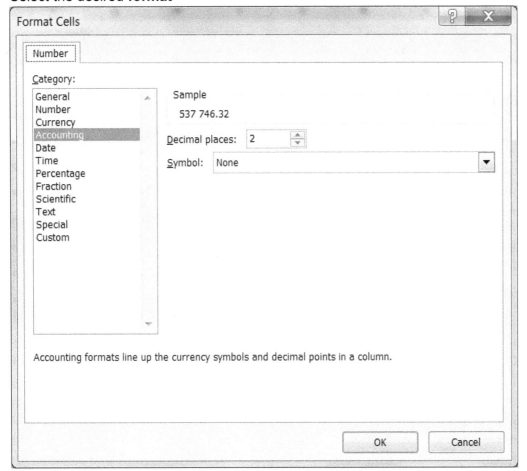

5. Select **OK**

Data Drill Down

You may be working with a PivotTable and need to see further details of an amount in the Data area. Often when a PivotTable is sent out, it is sent without the source data to ensure that there is no modification of the source data.

Method

1. In the **Data Area** of the **PivotTable**, **double click** on the **amount** you are wanting to drill into

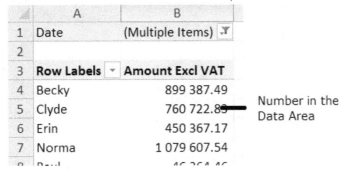

2. A **new worksheet** will be inserted with the details making up that amount from the **Data** area

Number	Name	Surname	Invoice Number	Amount Incl VAT	Amount Excl VAT	Date
9932	Ron	Grimes	INV 1582981	950497	833769.2982	16/12/1984

Calculated Fields

You can create your own calculated fields to include in your PivotTable but take note of the following important points

- You can use the same operators and expressions as you would in normal worksheet formulas
- You cannot use cell references or defined names

Method

1. From the **Options** tab, in the **Calculations** group, select **Fields, Items, & Sets**
2. Select **Calculated Field...** from the drop-down menu

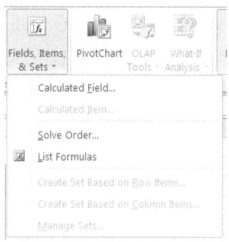

3. In the **Name box** enter the name

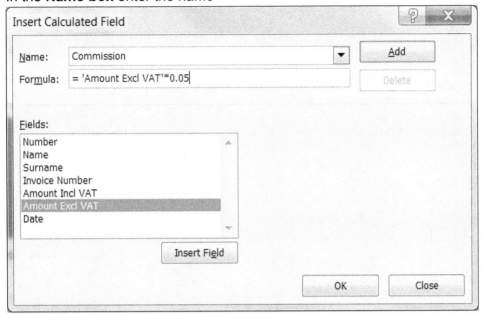

4. Select the field calculation: based on the **Fields List**
5. Select **Insert Field**
6. In the **Formula box**, edit the formula
7. Select **Add**
8. Select **OK**

Edit/Delete calculated field

Method

1. From the **Options** tab, in the **Calculations** group, select **Fields, Items, & Sets**
2. Select **Calculated Field…** from the drop-down menu

3. In the **Name box** select the drop-down arrow and select the field you would like to **edit/delete**

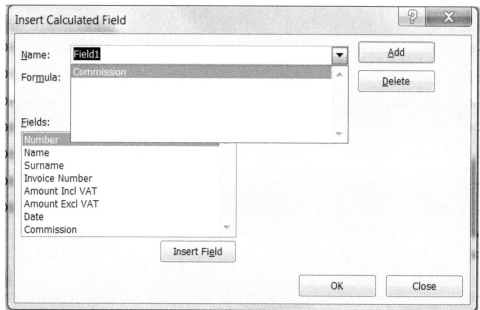

4. Make the necessary changes or press **Delete**
5. Select **OK**

Changes to the Location/Area of the Source Data

If you have added an extra column to the outside of the initially selected range, you will need to re-select the PivotTable area.

Method

1. Select any cell in the PivotTable
2. From the Options tab, in the Data group, select Change Data Source

3. Select the **collapse** button and re-select the data range

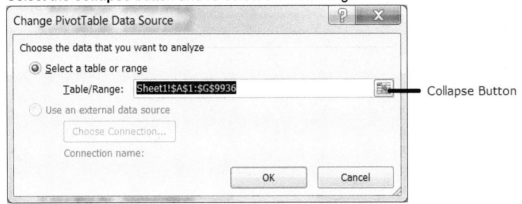

Collapse Button

4. Select **OK**

It is possible to consolidate Data and PivotTables using the Consolidate Tool:

*From the **Data** tab, in the **Data Tools** group, select **Consolidate***

*Select the first range for the **PivotTable**, select **Add***

*Select **additional** ranges*

*Select **OK***

Exercise: PivotTables

Open file: ***PivotTables.xlsx***

Steps

- Select any cell **within** the data on the **Sales** worksheet
- Click on [**Insert**][**Tables**][**PivotTable**]
- Click **OK** on the Create **PivotTable** dialog box
- Select the applicable fields as follows:

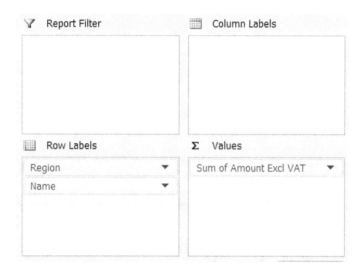

- Your results should be similar to:

Row Labels	Sum of Amount Excl VAT
⊟ **Head Office**	**1605663569**
Aaron Brandon	674662.6491
Aaron Li	1009981.86
Aaron Moody	1026387.228
Aaron Pugh	1146440.079
Adam Butler	742851.4474

- Select the **Value Field Settings...** of the **Amount Excl VAT** field
- Change the name to **Sales** and the number format to **Accounting** with **no symbol**
- **Center** align the **Sales** heading

Row Labels	Sales
⊟ **Head Office**	**1 605 663 568.89**
Aaron Brandon	674 662.65
Aaron Li	1 009 981.86
Aaron Moody	1 026 387.23
Aaron Pugh	1 146 440.08

- Sort the **Sales** data from **highest** to **lowest** values
- Then collapse the **Region** headings
- Apply any **PivotTable style** to your **PivotTable**

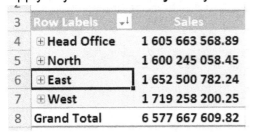

3	Row Labels ⬇	Sales
4	⊞ Head Office	1 605 663 568.89
5	⊞ North	1 600 245 058.45
6	⊞ East	1 652 500 782.24
7	⊞ West	1 719 258 200.25
8	Grand Total	6 577 667 609.82

- Click on **[PivotTable Tools Options][Calculations][Fields, Items & Sets][Calculated Field]**

  Name: **Cost Price**
  Formula: **='Amount Excl VAT'/125*100** (Remember to double click on **Amount Excl VAT** to use it, **don't retype it**)

- Format the heading the same as for **Sales** (Field name **Cost Price**, remember to add a **space** as this name already exist)

Row Labels ⬇	Sales	Cost Price
⊞ Head Office	1 605 663 568.89	1 284 530 855.11
⊞ North	1 600 245 058.45	1 280 196 046.76
⊞ East	1 652 500 782.24	1 322 000 625.79
⊞ West	1 719 258 200.25	1 375 406 560.20
Grand Total	6 577 667 609.82	5 262 134 087.86

- Click on **[PivotTable Tools Options][Fields, Items & Sets][Calculated Field]**

  Name: **Gross Profit**
  Formula: **='Amount Excl VAT' -'Cost Price'** (Remember to double click on **Amount Excl VAT** and **Cost Price** to use it, don't retype it)

- Format the heading the same as for **Sales**

Row Labels ↓	Sales	Cost Price	Gross Profit
⊞ Head Office	1 605 663 568.89	1 284 530 855.11	321 132 713.78
⊞ North	1 600 245 058.45	1 280 196 046.76	320 049 011.69
⊞ East	1 652 500 782.24	1 322 000 625.79	330 500 156.45
⊞ West	1 719 258 200.25	1 375 406 560.20	343 851 640.05
Grand Total	6 577 667 609.82	5 262 134 087.86	1 315 533 521.96

- Double click an **amount** in the **Head Office** line, you should get a new worksheet with only the **Head Office** data

	A	B	C	D	E	F	G
1	Number ▾	Name ▾	Invoice Number ▾	Amount Incl VAT ▾	Amount Excl VAT ▾	Date ▾	Region ▾
2	3135	Aaron Brandon	INV 1736907	769115.42	674662.6491	27/07/2003	Head Office
3	3198	Aaron Li	INV 1128316	1151379.32	1009981.86	25/05/2003	Head Office
4	6329	Aaron Moody	INV 1356165	1170081.44	1026387.228	28/10/1994	Head Office
5	7577	Aaron Pugh	INV 1924662	1306941.69	1146440.079	29/05/1991	Head Office
6	8982	Adam Butler	INV 1588452	846850.65	742851.4474	24/07/1987	Head Office
7	7430	Adam Bynum	INV 1899660	368618.54	323349.5965	23/10/1991	Head Office
8	4444	Adam Mayo	INV 1965887	197984.99	173671.0439	26/12/1999	Head Office
9	273	Adam Washington	INV 1057049	630547.16	553111.5439	28/05/2011	Head Office
10	3591	Alan Howell	INV 1627382	942969.44	827166.1754	27/04/2002	Head Office
11	463	Alan Levin	INV 1871628	193898.41	170086.3246	19/11/2010	Head Office
12	2789	Alan Meadows	INV 1001286	210196.93	184383.2719	07/07/2004	Head Office
13	5536	Alan Pollard	INV 1581993	1326485.46	1163583.737	29/12/1996	Head Office
14	1016	Alan Reilly	INV 1061179	1082218.52	949314.4912	15/05/2009	Head Office
15	3058	Alan Sutton	INV 1197333	1029817.94	903349.0702	12/10/2003	Head Office
16	9853	Albert Wiley	INV 1992577	620592.26	544379.1754	05/03/1985	Head Office
17	2582	Alex Ball	INV 1749653	587992.23	515782.6579	30/01/2005	Head Office

Hyperlinks

A hyperlink is a link from a worksheet that goes to another worksheet or file when you select it. You can hyperlink to any file, not just an Excel workbook. The hyperlink itself can be text or a picture. Hyperlinks can also link to e-mail addresses or websites.

Method

1. Select the **item** that you would like to create the **hyperlink** on
2. From the **Insert** tab in the **Links** group, select **Hyperlink**

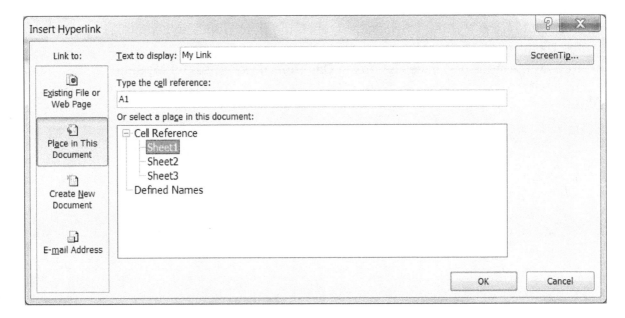

3. To hyperlink to another worksheet in the workbook, select **Place in This Document**
4. Under **Cell Reference**, select the **worksheet** you would like to link to
5. Under **Defined Names**, select any **named ranges** that you would like to link to
6. On the top right, select **Screen Tip** and enter in any **guidelines** you need to give
7. Select **OK**

---

*To quickly **insert**, **edit** or **remove** a **hyperlink**, **right** click on the item and select the desired option.*

Exercise: Hyperlinks

Open file: ***Hyperlinks.xlsx***

Steps

- Select the **Dashboard** worksheet
- Select cell **B3** and enter **MySheet 1**
- Select cell **B4** and enter **MySheet 2**
- Right click on cell **B3** and add a **hyperlink** to the **MySheet 1** worksheet
- **Click** on the hyperlink in cell **B3**, it should navigate you to the **MySheet 1** worksheet
- In cell **A1** on the **MySheet 1** worksheet, enter the word **Home** and create a **hyperlink** back to the **Dashboard** worksheet
- **Repeat** the steps now in cell **B4** on the **Dashboard** worksheet for **MySheet 2**

Solution

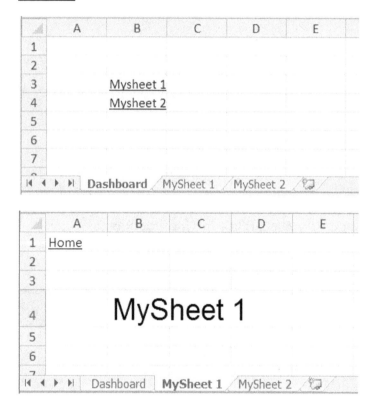

	A	B	C	D	E
1	Home				
2					
3					
4		MySheet 2			
5					
6					

Dashboard / MySheet 1 / **MySheet 2**

Text Functions

LEFT Function

LEFT returns the first characters in a text string, based on the number of characters you specify. In other words, you can specify the number of characters you want to be returned from the left-hand side of a text string.

Syntax:	=LEFT(text, [num_chars])
Text	Required. The text string that contains the characters you want to extract.
Num_chars	Optional. Specifies the number of characters you want **LEFT** to extract. • **Num_chars** must be greater than or equal to zero. • If **num_chars** is greater than the length of the text, **LEFT** returns all of the text. • If **num_chars** is omitted, it is assumed to be 1.

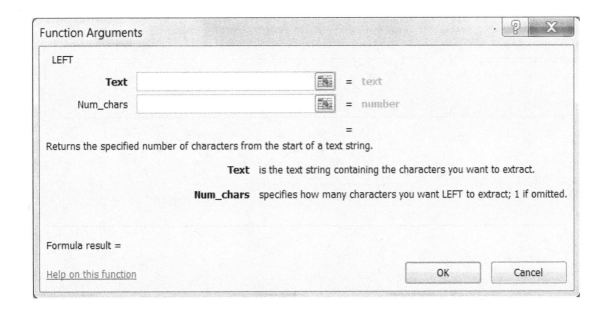

Method

1. Start the formula by typing an equal (=) sign in the cell followed by **LEFT** and an open bracket
=LEFT(....
2. Excel will then prompt you to complete the variables. Optional Variables will be shown in square brackets

OR

1. On the **Formulas** tab, in the **Function Library** group, click **Text**
2. **Select** the **LEFT** function
3. Complete the dialog box as shown above

OR

1. **Click** on the **Insert Function** button

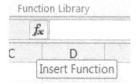

2. On the **Insert Function** dialog box, select the **Text** category, then select the **Left** function from the list of functions

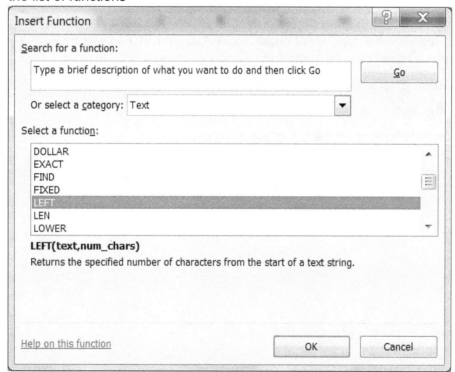

3. Click **OK**
4. Complete the **LEFT** dialog box as shown above

The **RIGHT** function works the same as the **LEFT** function it just returns characters from the right-hand side of a text string.

MID Function

MID returns a specific number of characters from a text string, starting at the position you specify, based on the number of characters you specify.

Syntax:	=MID(text, start_num, num_chars)
Text	Required. The text string that contains the characters you want to extract.
Start_num	Required. The position of the first character you want to extract in the text. The first character in the text has **start_num** 1, and so on.
Num_chars	Required. Specifies the number of characters you want MID to return from the text.

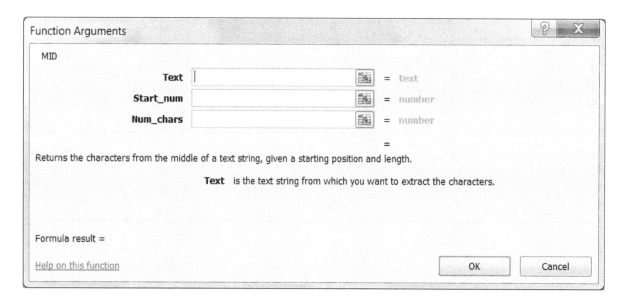

Method

1. Start the formula by typing an equal (=) sign in the cell followed by **MID** and an open bracket **=MID(…**
2. Excel will then prompt you to complete the variables. Optional Variables will be shown in square brackets

OR

1. On the **Formulas** tab, in the **Function Library** group, click **Text**
2. **Select** the **MID** function
3. Complete the dialog box as shown above

OR

1. **Click** on the **Insert Function** button

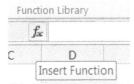

2. On the **Insert Function** dialog box, select the **Text** category, then select the **MID** function from the list of functions

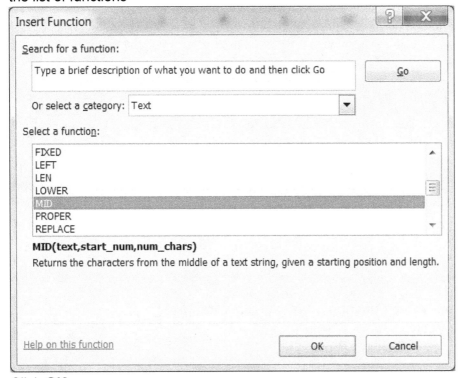

3. Click **OK**
4. Complete the **MID** dialog box as shown above

FIND Function

FIND locate one text string within a second text string, and return the number of the starting position of the first text string from the first character of the second text string.

Syntax:	= FIND(find_text, within_text, [start_num])
Find_text	Required. The text you want to find.
Within_text	Required. The text containing the text you want to find.
Start_num	Optional. Specifies the character at which to start the search. The first character in **within_text** is character number 1. If you omit **start_num**, it is assumed to be 1

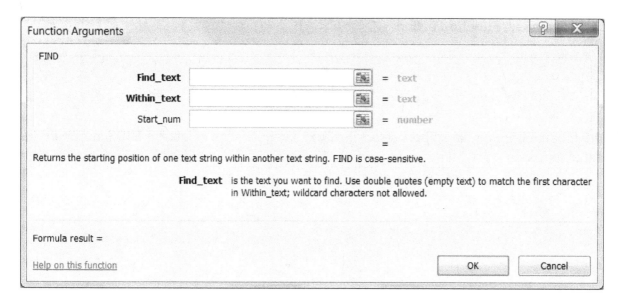

Method

1. Start the formula by typing an equal (=) sign in the cell followed by **FIND** and an open bracket **=FIND(...**
2. Excel will then prompt you to complete the variables. Optional Variables will be shown in square brackets

OR

1. On the **Formulas** tab, in the **Function Library** group, click **Text**
2. **Select** the **FIND** function
3. Complete the dialog box as shown above

OR

1. **Click** on the **Insert Function** button

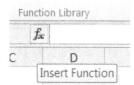

2. On the **Insert Function** dialog box, select the **Text** category, then select the **FIND** function from the list of functions

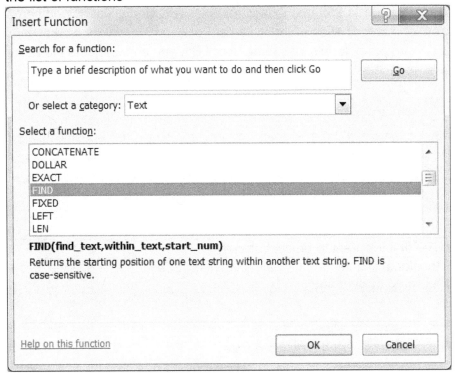

3. Click **OK**
4. Complete the **FIND** dialog box as shown above

Note: the **FIND** function is cAsE sEnSiTiVe.

CONCATENATE Function

The **CONCATENATE** function joins up to 255 text strings into one text string. The joined items can be text, numbers, cell references, or a combination of those items. For example, if your worksheet contains a person's first name in cell A1 and the person's last name in cell B1, you can combine the two values in another cell by using the following formula:

=CONCATENATE(A1," ",B1)

The second argument in this example (" ") is a space character. You must specify any spaces or punctuation that you want to appear in the results as an argument that is enclosed in quotation marks.

Syntax1:	= CONCATENATE(text1, [text2], ...)
Syntax2:	= text1 & " " & text2
Text1	Required. The first text item to be concatenated.
Text2,...	Optional. Additional text items, up to a maximum of 255 items. The items must be separated by commas.

If you use Syntax2 (**&**), the text must be placed in double quotes.

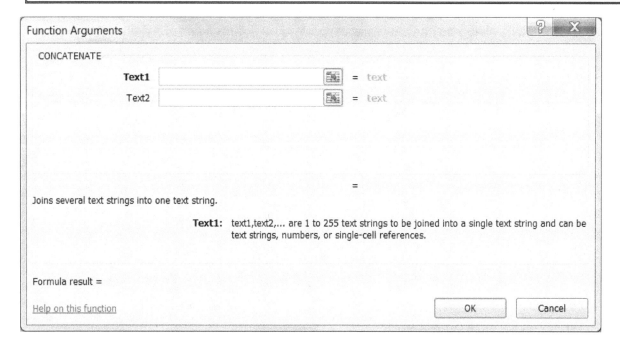

Method

1. Start the formula by typing an equal (**=**) sign in the cell followed by **CONCATENATE** and an open bracket **= CONCATENATE (...**
2. Excel will then prompt you to complete the variables. Optional Variables will be shown in square brackets

OR

1. On the **Formulas** tab, in the **Function Library** group, click **Text**
2. **Select** the CONCATENATE function
3. Complete the dialog box as shown above

OR

1. **Click** on the **Insert Function** button

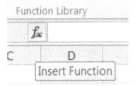

2. On the **Insert Function** dialog box, select the **Text** category, then select the **CONCATENATE** function from the list of functions

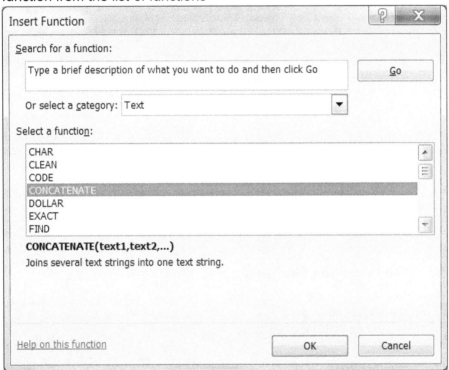

3. Click **OK**
4. Complete the **CONCATENATE** dialog box as shown above

TRIM Function

TRIM removes all spaces from text except for single spaces between words. Use **TRIM** on the text that you have received from another application that may have irregular spacing.

Syntax1:	= TRIM(text)

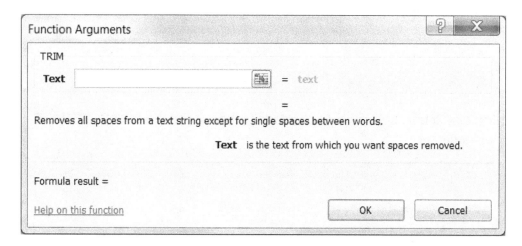

Method

1. Start the formula by typing an equal (=) sign in the cell followed by **TRIM** and an open bracket
   = TRIM (...
2. Excel will then prompt you to complete the variables. Optional Variables will be shown in square brackets

OR

1. On the **Formulas** tab, in the **Function Library** group, click **Text**
2. **Select** the **TRIM** function
3. Complete the dialog box as shown above

OR

1. **Click** on the **Insert Function** button

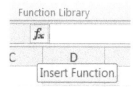

2. On the **Insert Function** dialog box, select the **Text** category, then select the **TRIM** function from the list of functions
3. Click **OK**
4. Complete the **TRIM** dialog box as shown above

LEN Function

LEN returns the number of characters in a text string.

Syntax1:	= LEN(text)

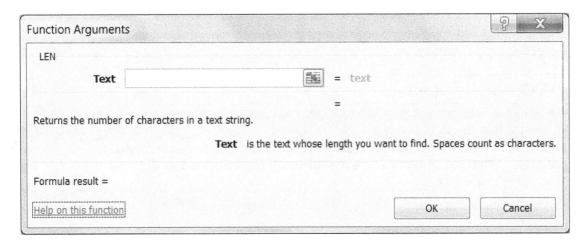

Method

1. Start the formula by typing an equal (=) sign in the cell followed by **LEN** and an open bracket **= LEN (...**
2. Excel will then prompt you to complete the variables. Optional Variables will be shown in square brackets

OR

1. On the **Formulas** tab, in the **Function Library** group, click **Text**
2. **Select** the **LEN** function
3. Complete the dialog box as shown above

OR

1. **Click** on the **Insert Function** button

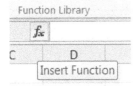

2. On the **Insert Function** dialog box, select the **Text** category, then select the **LEN** function from the list of functions
3. Click **OK**
4. Complete the **LEN** dialog box as shown above

TEXT Function

The **TEXT** function converts a numeric value to text and lets you specify the display formatting by using special format strings. This function is useful in situations where you want to display numbers in a more readable format, or you want to combine numbers with text or symbols. For example, suppose cell A1 contains the date 23 April 2013. To format the date as a day word, you can use the following formula:

=TEXT(A1,"dddd")

In this example, Excel displays **Tuesday**.

Syntax1:	=TEXT(value, format_text)
Value	Required. A numeric value, a formula that evaluates to a numeric value, or a reference to a cell containing a numeric value.
Format_text	Required. A numeric format as a text string enclosed in quotation marks, for example, "dddd" or "mmmm". See the following sections for specific formatting guidelines

m	Displays the month as a number without a leading zero.
mm	Displays the month as a number with a leading zero when appropriate.
mmm	Displays the month as an abbreviation (Jan to Dec).
mmmm	Displays the month as a full name (January to December).
mmmmm	Displays the month as a single letter (J to D).
d	Displays the day as a number without a leading zero.
dd	Displays the day as a number with a leading zero when appropriate.
ddd	Displays the day as an abbreviation (Sun to Sat).
dddd	Displays the day as a full name (Sunday to Saturday).
yy	Displays the year as a two-digit number.
yyyy	Displays the year as a four-digit number.

> *In these examples the **date** formatting was used, you can use **any** cell formatting available in Excel in this function.*

Exercise: Text Functions

Open file: *Text Functions.xlsx*

On the **Invoice List** sheet

<u>**Steps**</u>

Obtain the document type

- Enter a **LEFT** function in cell **C2**. You can either type it in or use the **function libraries** and **dialog box**

text	A2
num_chars	3

- The answer you get should be the **first 3** letters **INV**
- Use either the **Fill** handle or **Copy & Paste** to **copy** the formula up to cell **C30**

Obtain the invoice number

- Enter a **RIGHT** function in cell **D2**. You can either type it in or use the **function libraries** and **dialog box**

text	A2
num_chars	5

- The answer you get should be the **last 5** numbers of the invoice
- Use either the **Fill** handle or **Copy & Paste** to **copy** the formula up to cell **D30**

Obtain the system the invoice was created from

- Enter a **MID** function in cell **E2**. You can either type it in or use the **function libraries** and **dialog box**

text	A2
start_num	4
num_chars	1

- The answer you get should be the either **A** or **B** depending on the invoice number
- Use either the **Fill** handle or **Copy & Paste** to copy the formula up to cell **E30**

Get the day of the week the invoice was generated

- Enter a **TEXT** function in cell **F2**. You can either type it in or use the **function libraries** and **dialog box**

value	B2

format_text	"dddd"

- The answer you get should be a **day** of the week
- Use either the **Fill** handle or **Copy & Paste** to copy the formula up to cell **F30**

On the **Customers** sheet

<u>**Steps**</u>

Get the length of the Customer text

- Enter a **LEN** function in cell **B2**. You can either type it in or use the **function libraries** and **dialog box**

text	A2

- The answer you get should be the **length** of the **customer** field
- Use either the **Fill** handle or **Copy & Paste** to copy the formula up to cell **B9**

Find the location of the first space in the Customer field

- Enter a **FIND** function in cell **C2**. You can either type it in or use the **function libraries** and **dialog box**

find_text	" "
within_text	A2

- The answer should be the **location** of the **space** in the customer field
- Use either the **Fill** handle or **Copy & Paste** to copy the formula up to cell **C9**

Get the surname value from the customer field

- Enter a **RIGHT** function in cell **D2**. You can either type it in or use the **function libraries** and **dialog box**

text	A2
num_chars	B2-C2

- The answer you get should be the **surnames** only
- Use either the **Fill** handle or **Copy & Paste** to copy the formula up to cell **D9**

Get the length of the surname field (Column D)

- Enter a **LEN** function in cell **E2**. You can either type it in or use the **function libraries** and **dialog box**

text	D2

- The answer you get should be the **length** of the **surname** value
- Use either the **Fill** handle or **Copy & Paste** to copy the formula up to cell **E9**

Get the name value from the customer field

- Enter a **LEFT** function in cell **F2**. You can either type it in or use the **function libraries** and **dialog box**

text	A2
num_chars	B2-E2-1

(The extra 1 subtracted here is to exclude the **space** between the name and surname, you could also use **TRIM** here)

- The answer you get should be the **names** only
- Use either the **Fill** handle or **Copy & Paste** to copy the formula up to cell **F9**

Putting it all together

Get the surname value from the customer field

- Enter a **RIGHT** function in cell **I2**. You can either type it in or use the **function libraries** and **dialog box**

text	A2
num_chars	LEN(A2)-FIND(" ",A2)

- The answer you get should be the **surnames** only
- Use either the **Fill** handle or **Copy & Paste** to copy the formula up to cell **I9**

Get the name value from the customer field

- Enter a **LEFT** function in cell **H2**. You can either type it in or use the **function libraries** and **dialog box**

text	A2
num_chars	LEN(A2)-LEN(I2)-1

- The answer you get should be the **names** only
- Use either the **Fill** handle or **Copy & Paste** to copy the formula up to cell **H9**

On the **Addresses** sheet

Steps

Combine the address parts to form a complete address

- Enter a **CONCATENATE** function in cell **E2**. You can either type it in or use the **function libraries** and **dialog box**

text	B2, " ", C2, ", ",D2

- The answer you get should be the **combined address**
- Use either the **Fill** handle or **Copy & Paste** to copy the formula up to cell **E9**

Solution

Invoice List

	A	B	C	D	E	F
1	Invoice Number	Date	Doc type	Number	System	Day
2	INVA23094	26/02/2013	INV	23094	A	Tuesday
3	INVB23095	27/02/2013	INV	23095	B	Wednesday
4	INVA23096	28/02/2013	INV	23096	A	Thursday
5	INVA23097	01/03/2013	INV	23097	A	Friday

Customers

	A	B	C	D	E	F	G	H	I
1	Customer	Length (Customer)	Find space	Surname (RIGHT)	Length (Surname)	Name (LEFT)		Name	Surname
2	Alex Durand	11	5	Durand	6	Alex		Alex	Durand
3	Al Li	5	3	Li	2	Al		Al	Li
4	Johannes van der Westhuizen	27	9	van der Westhuizen	18	Johannes		Johannes	van der Westhuizen

Addresses

	A	B	C	D	E
1	Customer	Street Number	Street	Town	Address
2	Alex Durand	22	Church Street	Durban	22 Church Street, Durban
3	Al Gore	135	Columbine Avenue	Roodepoort	135 Columbine Avenue, Roodepoort
4	Johannes van der Westhuizen	5	Long Street	Cape Town	5 Long Street, Cape Town
5	Pete Tallman	6598	Nelson Mandela Drive	Cape Town	6598 Nelson Mandela Drive, Cape Town
6	Wesley Johnson	652	Main Street	Pretoria	652 Main Street, Pretoria
7	Kyle Peters	65	Protea Avenue	Germiston	65 Protea Avenue, Germiston
8	Yolandie Ferreira	24	Michelle Avenue	Alberton	24 Michelle Avenue, Alberton
9	Richard Holbrook	253	William Nicol Drive	Fourways	253 William Nicol Drive, Fourways

Working with Data Lists

A data list is simply a list of data that has been entered in a series of rows with no blank rows in between. Excel can then easily manage the data in many different ways by sorting, filtering, subtotaling and grouping. These are ways in which you may want to work with the data in the event that you do not want to use a PivotTable or cannot use one due to the limitation on the number of records you need to Pivot.

These tools are very useful and assist with the performance of your work.

When working with a data list you should keep the following in mind:

- Never insert a blank row or column between your headings and your data otherwise they will not form part of the list
- Rather format the column and row headings in a different way to the actual data in the list as Excel can then easily detect if the list has row or column headings
- Don't place important information to the left or right of the list, this data could be hidden if you filter your data
- Any blank rows or columns will separate the data into separate data lists that operate independently from each other
- Unhide any hidden rows or columns before making changes to the list to prevent you from accidentally deleting them
- Spaces at the beginning or end of a cell will affect the sorting and search, format the cells with indents instead

Sorting Data

Sorting can either be done as a Single Level sort, where you sort only one column at a time or as a Multi-Level sort where you can sort up to 64 columns at the same time.

You can sort data by text (**A to Z** or **Z to A**), numbers (smallest to largest or largest to smallest), and dates and times (oldest to newest and newest to oldest) in one or more columns. You can also sort by a **custom list** (such as Large, Medium, and Small) or by **format**, including cell **colour**, **font** colour, or **icon** set. Most sort operations are column sorts, but you can also sort by rows.

Excel will sort data in the following manner in Ascending:

- (space)
- ! " # & %
- 0 1 2 3 4 5
- A B C D E F G H

Single Level Sorting

You can use single level sorting for sorting a single column in either ascending or descending order.

<u>Method</u>

1. Select a **cell** in the column you wish to sort
2. From the **Home** tab, in the **Editing** group, select **Sort & Filter**

3. Select **Sort A to Z** or **Sort Z to A**

Multi-Level Sorting

Multi-level sorting allows you to sort up to 64 columns at a time.

Method

1. Select any **cell** within the data list you wish to sort
2. From the **Data** tab, in the **Sort & Filter** group, select **Sort**
3. Select the **drop-down** arrow in the **Column** box and select the column you wish to sort

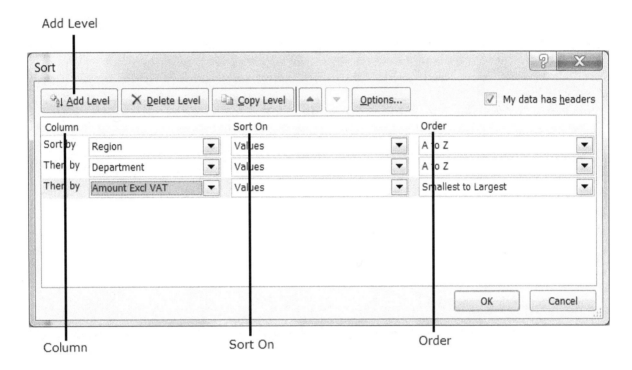

4. Select the **drop-down** arrow in the **Sort On** box and select the method you wish to sort by
5. Select the **drop-down** arrow in the **Order** box and select the sort order you wish to sort by
6. Select the **Add Level** button to specify the next sort column
7. Repeat steps **3** to **5**
8. Repeat steps **6** and **7** for subsequent columns
9. Select **OK**

Set a Custom Sort Order

The custom list feature allows the user to define a specific sort order. This means the user will be able to sort a list in which ever order specified, not necessarily alphabetical or numerical.

Method

1. On a **blank** Excel worksheet, enter the **sort order** (text) as you would want it to be sorted
2. Select the **list** you would like to base you **Custom List** on (as created in **step 1**)

3. Select the **Options** under the **File** tab

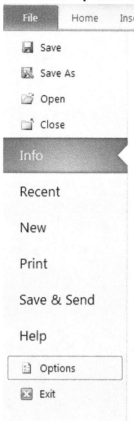

4. Select the **Advanced** category, then select the **Edit Custom Lists...** in the **General** grouping (near the end of the list)

Excel Options

General	**When calculating this workbook:**	⊠ Induction Excel File.... ▼
Formulas		
Proofing	☑ Update links to other documents	
Save	☐ Set precision as displayed	
	☐ Use 1904 date system	
Language	☑ Save external link values	
Advanced	**General**	
Customize Ribbon	☐ Provide feedback with sound	
Quick Access Toolbar	☑ Provide feedback with animation	
	☐ Ignore other applications that use Dynamic Data Exchange (DDE)	
Add-Ins	☑ Ask to update automatic links	
Trust Center	☐ Show add-in user interface errors	
	☑ Scale content for A4 or 8.5 x 11" paper sizes	
	☑ Show customer submitted Office.com content	

At startup, open all files in: [_____]

Web Options...

☑ Enable multi-threaded processing

☑ Disable undo for large PivotTable refresh operations to reduce refre

Disable undo for PivotTables with at least this number of data sourc

Create lists for use in sorts and fill sequences: Edit Custom Lists...

5. In the **Custom Lists** dialog box, select **Import**. The copied list is pasted into the **List entries** box

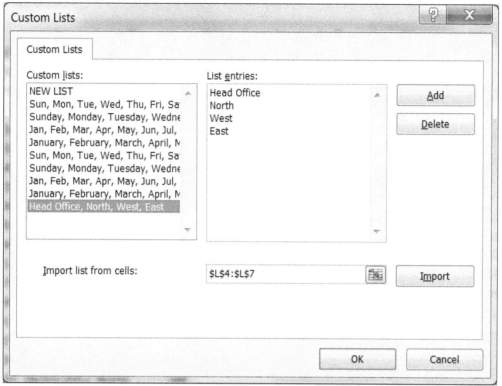

6. Select **OK**, **OK** (The list is added to the custom list entries)
7. Select a cell in the **column** that you are wanting to sort
8. From the **Data** tab, in the **Sort & Filter** group, select **Sort**
9. Select the **drop-down** arrow in the **Sort On** box and select the column you wish to sort
10. Select the **drop-down** arrow in the **Order** box and select **Custom List...**

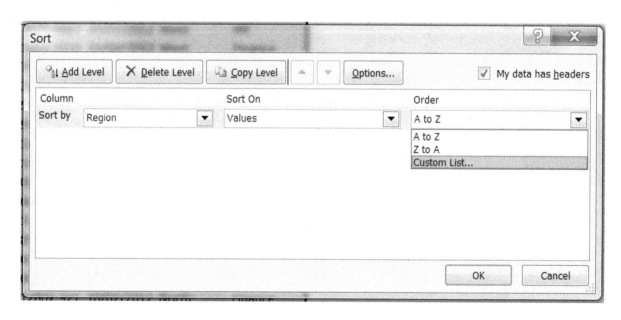

11. Select the specific custom list

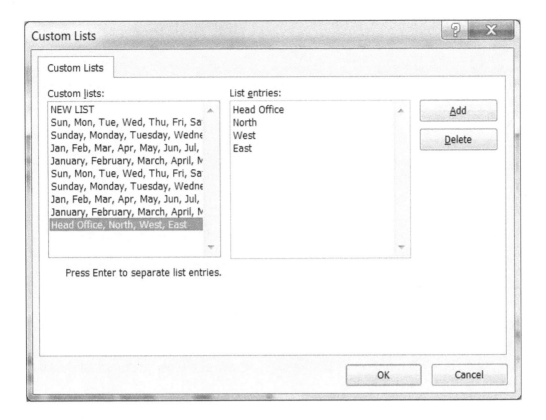

12. Select **OK, OK**
13. You can **delete** the custom list you created in **step 1**

---

*Note: This new **Custom Sort** order is not limited to a specific workbook; it will be available to you the next time you open another workbook as well.*

Sorting data by Rows

Sometimes you need to sort your data in rows instead of columns.

Method

1. *Select* the data you wish to sort (excluding the headers in the first column)
2. From the **Data** tab, in the **Sort & Filter** group, select **Sort**
3. Click on the **Options...** button

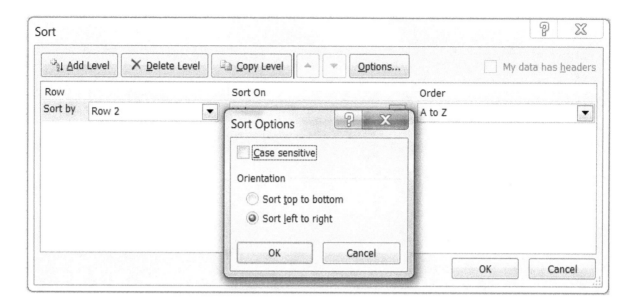

4. Select **Sort left to right**
5. Click **OK**
6. Now the **Sort** dialog box will function as before but you will see **Row** options instead of **Column** options
7. When you are done, click **OK** and your data should be sorted in the row or rows you specified

*Note: If you need to return your data to its **original** state (the sort order you received or created it in) then it is good practice to add an **extra counting column** so you can return the data to its original state by sorting on this column.*

Exercise: Sorting Data

Open file: ***Sorting Data.xlsx***

Steps

- Select any cell in the **Sales** column
- Click **[Data][Sort & Filter][A to Z]**

The lowest sales will now be on top

	A	B	C	D	E
1	#	City	Department	Date	Sales
2	40050	East London	Music	19 June 2012	60 000.14
3	26986	Johannesburg	Linen	10 December 2012	60 001.33
4	116754	Nelspruit	Clothing	20 January 2012	60 001.48
5	90795	East London	Household	08 November 2012	60 004.32
6	83762	Durban	IT	25 March 2012	60 004.97
7	28202	Pretoria	Linen	18 January 2012	60 005.66
8	89777	Pretoria	Household	23 February 2012	60 007.22
9	91240	East London	Linen	16 July 2012	60 007.52
10	939	East London	Household	16 July 2012	60 007.58
11	58080	Bloemfontein	IT	02 November 2012	60 008.46
12	43659	Johannesburg	Household	21 May 2012	60 008.48
13	92904	Nelspruit	Clothing	21 August 2012	60 009.07

- Select any cell in the data
- Click **[Data][Sort & Filter][Sort]**
- Sort the data by **Date** (Oldest to Newest) and then by **Sales** (Largest to Smallest)

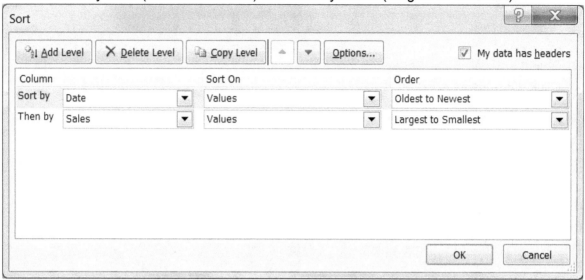

- Click **OK**

◢	A	B	C	D	E
1	**#**	**City**	**Department**	**Date**	**Sales**
2	17946	Nelspruit	Household	01 January 2012	149 861.25
3	65320	East London	Music	01 January 2012	148 488.65
4	21951	Kimberley	Clothing	01 January 2012	148 361.53
5	106262	Bloemfontein	Garden	01 January 2012	148 131.43
6	97110	East London	Gorceries	01 January 2012	147 715.36
7	82200	Cape Town	Gorceries	01 January 2012	147 235.17
8	942	George	Linen	01 January 2012	147 161.09
9	96004	Pretoria	Linen	01 January 2012	146 961.81
10	82799	Nelspruit	Linen	01 January 2012	146 182.72
11	91070	George	Linen	01 January 2012	146 011.89
12	84557	Kimberley	Linen	01 January 2012	145 320.24
13	69881	East London	Clothing	01 January 2012	145 311.02
14	7691	East London	Music	01 January 2012	145 056.72

- Select any cell in the data
- Click **[Data][Sort & Filter][Sort]**
- Sort the data by # (Cell colour - yellow) and then by # (Cell colour - green)

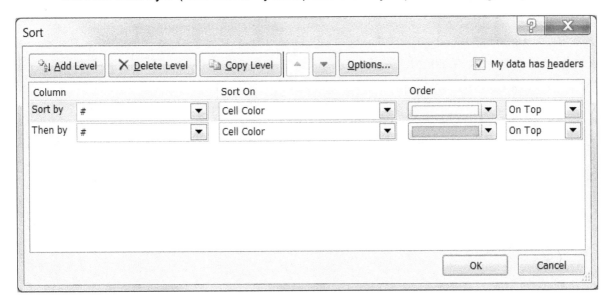

- Click **OK**

	A	B	C	D	E
1	**#**	**City**	**Department**	**Date**	**Sales**
2	100023	Durban	IT	08 January 2012	135 323.43
3	48509	Pretoria	Music	31 July 2012	86 027.47
4	327	Bloemfontein	Household	26 August 2012	125 545.03
5	121	Johannesburg	Gorceries	09 November 2012	121 718.49
6	3274	Nelspruit	Household	31 December 2012	127 850.05
7	119987	Cape Town	Gorceries	08 March 2012	111 518.78
8	12	Cape Town	Household	24 April 2012	132 323.89
9	115293	George	Household	20 June 2012	85 812.76
10	44476	East London	IT	30 July 2012	115 886.53
11	17946	Nelspruit	Household	01 January 2012	149 861.25
12	65320	East London	Music	01 January 2012	148 488.65
13	21951	Kimberley	Clothing	01 January 2012	148 361.53

Exercise: Custom Sort order

Open file: **Sorting Data.xlsx**

Steps

- Select any cell in the **City** column
- Click [**Data**][**Sort & Filter**][**A to Z**]

The data will now be sorted in the following alphabetical **City** order:

- o Bloemfontein
- o Cape Town
- o Durban
- o East London
- o George
- o Johannesburg
- o Kimberley
- o Nelspruit
- o Pretoria

	A	B	C	D	E
1	#	City	Department	Date	Sales
2	4	Bloemfontein	Household	24 March 2012	139 674.89
3	14	Bloemfontein	Clothing	12 September 2012	86 286.43
4	21	Bloemfontein	Household	06 October 2012	103 470.56
5	54	Bloemfontein	IT	06 June 2012	118 672.97
6	69	Bloemfontein	Garden	23 February 2012	106 922.06
7	72	Bloemfontein	Garden	09 September 2012	90 135.73
8	79	Bloemfontein	IT	25 May 2012	147 870.99
9	81	Bloemfontein	Clothing	08 May 2012	80 333.78
10	87	Bloemfontein	Garden	09 April 2012	70 257.89

Now we want to sort our data in the following **City** order (size of our branches):

- o Johannesburg
- o Pretoria
- o Cape Town
- o Durban
- o Bloemfontein
- o East London
- o Kimberley
- o Nelspruit
- o George

- Select **Sheet2** and **type** or **copy** the list in the **order** you **want**
- **Select** the list you just created

	A	B
1		
2		
3		
4		Johannesburg
5		Pretoria
6		Cape Town
7		Durban
8		Bloemfontein
9		East London
10		Kimberley
11		Nelspruit
12		George

- Click **[File][Options]**
- Select the **Advanced** tab
- **Scroll** to the **bottom** of the screen and select **Edit Custom Lists...** under the **General** heading

Create lists for use in sorts and fill sequences: **Edit Custom Lists...**

- Click on **Import**

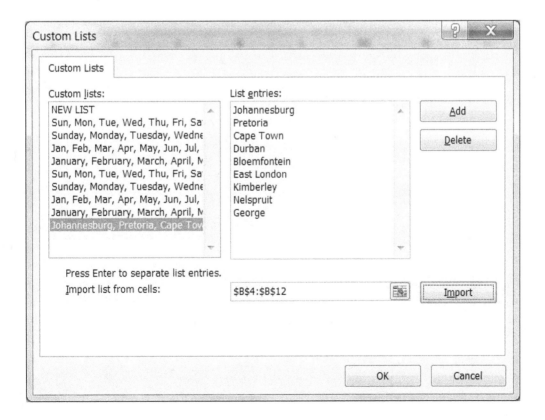

- Click on **OK**, **OK**

- Select any cell in the data
- Click [**Data**][**Sort & Filter**][**Sort**]
- In the order drop-down select **Custom List...**
- Select **your list** and click **OK**, **OK**
- The data is now sorted by **your City** order

	A	B	C	D	E
1	#	City	Department	Date	Sales
2	11	Johannesburg	Linen	13 November 2012	79 122.99
3	39	Johannesburg	Linen	11 January 2012	112 573.95
4	46	Johannesburg	IT	29 July 2012	101 816.47
5	63	Johannesburg	Household	24 August 2012	78 805.13
6	66	Johannesburg	Linen	27 April 2012	142 146.72
7	99	Johannesburg	Garden	03 December 2012	93 105.64
8	105	Johannesburg	Music	08 March 2012	124 850.11
9	106	Johannesburg	Household	02 November 2012	129 621.80

Subtotalling

You can automatically calculate subtotals and grand totals in a list for a column by using the Subtotal command.

Create Subtotals

Method

1. Select any **cell** in the data list
2. **Sort** the list by fields you want subtotals on
3. From the **Data** tab, in the **Outline** group, select **Subtotal**

4. Select the **drop-down** arrow in **the At each change in** box
5. Select the sorted column (the one on which the subtotals will be based)
6. Select the **drop-down** arrow in the **Use function** box
7. Select the **function** you want to use to calculate the subtotals, e.g. **SUM**
8. Select the check boxes to place a tick mark for the columns that you want subtotals created in the **Add subtotal to** box
9. Select **Replace current subtotals** if not already selected (This will replace any existing subtotals in the worksheet)
   If you are adding your **2nd level of subtotalling**, you will **de-select** this option in order to add the next level of subtotalling to the existing one
10. Select the **Summary below data** if not already selected (This will place the totals beneath each grouping and not above)
11. Select **OK**

You can now use the **Expand/Collapse** buttons the filter the data

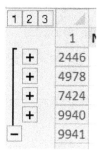

Remove all Subtotals

Method

1. Select any **cell** in the list
2. From the **Data** tab, in the **Outline** group, select **Subtotal**
3. Select **Remove All**
4. Select **OK**

Copying Subtotals

If you use normal copy and paste, you will copy all the hidden information as well as the subtotals, but there is a way of copying just the subtotals as displayed.

Method

1. **Apply** the necessary **subtotals**
2. **Summarise** your data by selecting the relevant **level**
3. Select the **range** of cells
4. From the **Home** tab, in the **Editing** group, select **Find & Select**

5. Select **Go To Special...**

6. Under **Select**, select **Visible cells only**

7. Select **OK**
8. From the **Home** tab, in the **Clipboard** group, select **Copy**
9. Select the position you want to copy to
10. From the **Home** tab, in the **Clipboard** group, select **Paste**

Exercise: Subtotalling

Open file: **Subtotalling.xlsx**

Steps

- Add a **multi-level sort** on the data on the **Data** worksheet. Sort by **Region** and then **Department**
- Click on **[Data][Outline][Subtotal]**
- Select the following options:

At each change in **Region**
Use function: **Sum**
Add subtotal to **Amount Incl VAT** and **Amount Excl VAT**
Replace current subtotals

- Click **OK**
- Click on **[Data][Outline][Subtotal]** again

- Select the following options:

At each change in **Department**
Use function: **Sum**
Add subtotal to **Amount Incl VAT** and **Amount Excl VAT**
Replace current subtotals NOT SELECTED

- Click **OK**
- Click on the **third** level of subtotalling

Solution

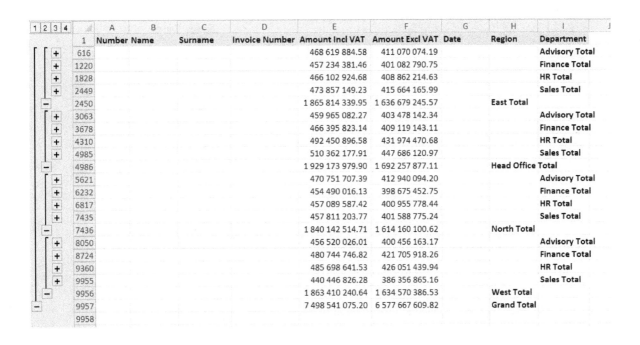

1 2 3 4		A	B	C	D	E	F	G	H	I	J
	1	Number	Name	Surname	Invoice Number	Amount Incl VAT	Amount Excl VAT	Date	Region	Department	
+	616					468 619 884.58	411 070 074.19			Advisory Total	
+	1220					457 234 381.46	401 082 790.75			Finance Total	
+	1828					466 102 924.68	408 862 214.63			HR Total	
+	2449					473 857 149.23	415 664 165.99			Sales Total	
−	2450					1 865 814 339.95	1 636 679 245.57		East Total		
+	3063					459 965 082.27	403 478 142.34			Advisory Total	
+	3678					466 395 823.14	409 119 143.11			Finance Total	
+	4310					492 450 896.58	431 974 470.68			HR Total	
+	4985					510 362 177.91	447 686 120.97			Sales Total	
−	4986					1 929 173 979.90	1 692 257 877.11		Head Office Total		
+	5621					470 751 707.39	412 940 094.20			Advisory Total	
+	6232					454 490 016.13	398 675 452.75			Finance Total	
+	6817					457 089 587.42	400 955 778.44			HR Total	
+	7435					457 811 203.77	401 588 775.24			Sales Total	
−	7436					1 840 142 514.71	1 614 160 100.62		North Total		
+	8050					456 520 026.01	400 456 163.17			Advisory Total	
+	8724					480 744 746.82	421 705 918.26			Finance Total	
+	9360					485 698 641.53	426 051 439.94			HR Total	
+	9955					440 446 826.28	386 356 865.16			Sales Total	
−	9956					1 863 410 240.64	1 634 570 386.53		West Total		
−	9957					7 498 541 075.20	6 577 667 609.82		Grand Total		
	9958										

Copy the displayed results to Sheet2

Steps

- **Select** the data you wish to copy
- Click on [**Home**][**Editing**][**Find & Select**][**Go To Special…**]
- Select Visible cells only
- Click **OK**
- Click on [**Home**][**Clipboard**][**Copy**]
- Select cell **A1** on **Sheet2**
- Click on [**Home**][**Clipboard**][**Paste**]

Solution

	A	B	C	D	E
1	Amount Incl VAT	Amount Excl VAT	Date	Region	Department
2	468 619 884.58	411 070 074.19			Advisory Total
3	457 234 381.46	401 082 790.75			Finance Total
4	466 102 924.68	408 862 214.63			HR Total
5	473 857 149.23	415 664 165.99			Sales Total
6	1 865 814 339.95	1 636 679 245.57		East Total	
7	459 965 082.27	403 478 142.34			Advisory Total
8	466 395 823.14	409 119 143.11			Finance Total
9	492 450 896.58	431 974 470.68			HR Total
10	510 362 177.91	447 686 120.97			Sales Total
11	1 929 173 979.90	1 692 257 877.11		Head Office Total	
12	470 751 707.39	412 940 094.20			Advisory Total
13	454 490 016.13	398 675 452.75			Finance Total
14	457 089 587.42	400 955 778.44			HR Total
15	457 811 203.77	401 588 775.24			Sales Total
16	1 840 142 514.71	1 614 160 100.62		North Total	
17	456 520 026.01	400 456 163.17			Advisory Total
18	480 744 746.82	421 705 918.26			Finance Total
19	485 698 641.53	426 051 439.94			HR Total
20	440 446 826.28	386 356 865.16			Sales Total
21	1 863 410 240.64	1 634 570 386.53		West Total	
22	7 498 541 075.20	6 577 667 609.82		Grand Total	

SUBTOTAL Function

The **SUBTOTAL** function returns a subtotal in a list or database. The **SUBTOTAL** function is very useful when you are filtering your list and wanting to calculate the filtered fields.

Syntax:	=SUBTOTAL(function_num,ref1,[ref2],...])
function_num	Required. The number 1 to 11 (includes hidden values) or 101 to 111 (ignores hidden values) that specifies which function to use in calculating subtotals within a list. (**9** is most commonly used – **SUM**)
ref1	Required. The first named range or reference for which you want the subtotal.
ref2, …	Optional. Named ranges or references 2 to 254 for which you want the subtotal.

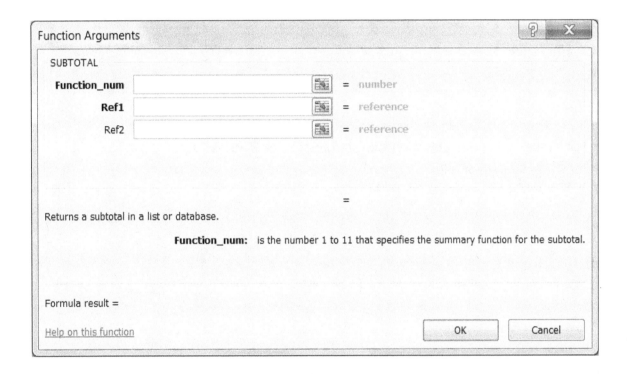

Function_num (includes hidden values)	Function_num (ignores hidden values)	Function
1	101	AVERAGE
2	102	COUNT
3	103	COUNTA
4	104	MAX
5	105	MIN
6	106	PRODUCT
7	107	STDEV
8	108	STDEVP
9	109	SUM

| 10 | 110 | VAR |
| 11 | 111 | VARP |

> Note: If there are other **subtotals** within **ref1**, **ref2**, … (or nested **subtotals**), these nested **subtotals** are ignored to avoid double counting.

Method

1. Start the formula by typing an equal (=) sign in the cell followed by **SUBTOTAL** and an open bracket **=SUBTOTAL(**...
2. Excel will then prompt you to complete the variables. Optional Variables will be shown in square brackets

> If you type the **SUBTOTAL** formula, you will get a drop-down list from which you can select the function number/calculation method.

OR

1. On the **Formulas** tab, in the **Function Library** group, click **Math & Trig**
2. **Select** the **SUBTOTAL** function
3. Complete the dialog box as shown above

OR

1. **Click** on the **Insert Function** button

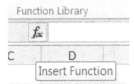

2. On the **Insert Function** dialog box, select the **Math & Trig** category, then select the **SUBTOTAL** function from the list of functions

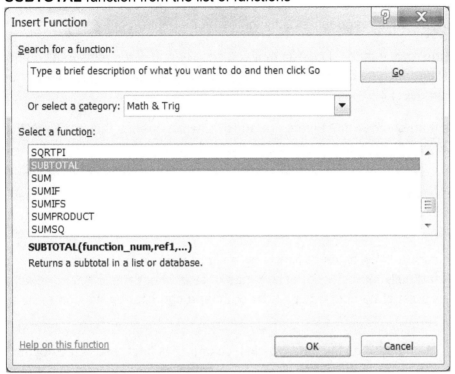

3. Click **OK**
4. Complete the **SUBTOTAL** dialog box as shown above

Filtering Data

Filtering data is a quick and easy way to find and work with a subset of data in a range of cells or table. For example, you can filter to see only the values that you specify, filter to see the top or bottom values or filter to quickly see duplicate values.

After you have filtered data in a range of cells or table, you can either reapply a filter to get up-to-date results or clear a filter to redisplay all of the data. Filtering doesn't change your data in any way. As soon as you remove the filter, all your data reappear, exactly the same as before.

Filtered data displays only the rows that meet criteria that you specify and hides rows that you don't want to be displayed. After you filter data, you can copy, find, edit, format, chart, and print the subset of filtered data without rearranging or moving it.

You can also filter by more than one column. Filters are additive, which means that each additional filter is based on the current filter and further reduces the subset of data that is shown.

> *Note: When you use the **Find** dialog box to search filtered data, only the data that is displayed is searched; data that is not displayed is not searched. To search all the data, clear all filters.*

Using **AutoFilter**, you can create three types of filters: by a list of **values**, by a **format**, or by **criteria**. Each of these filter types is mutually exclusive for each range of cells or column table. For example, you can filter by cell colour or by a list of numbers, but not by both; you can filter by an icon or by a custom filter, but not by both.

Excel will give you filtering option based on the data type in a column. For best results, do not mix storage formats, such as text and number or number and date, in the same column because only one type of filter command is available for each column. If there is a mix of storage formats in a column, the command that is displayed is the storage format that occurs the most. For example, if the column contains three values stored as a number and four as text, the filter command that is displayed is **Text Filters**.

Filter Options

Number Filter	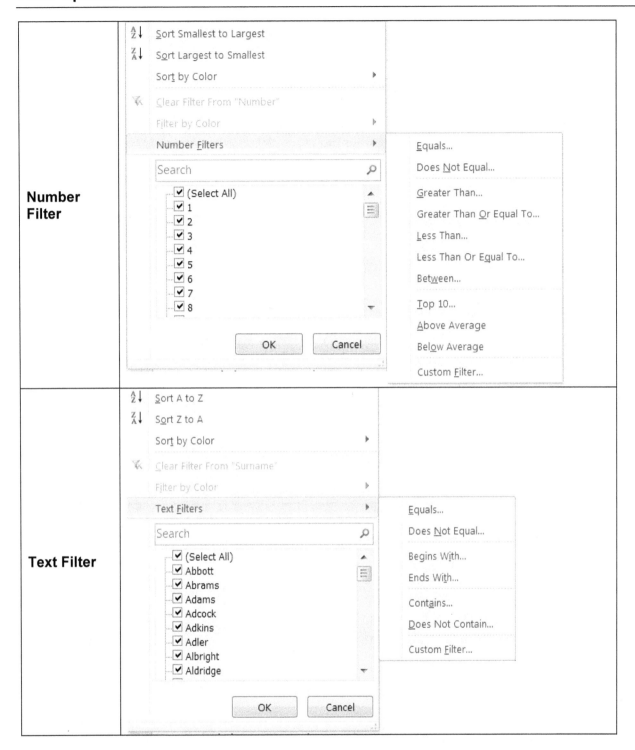
Text Filter	

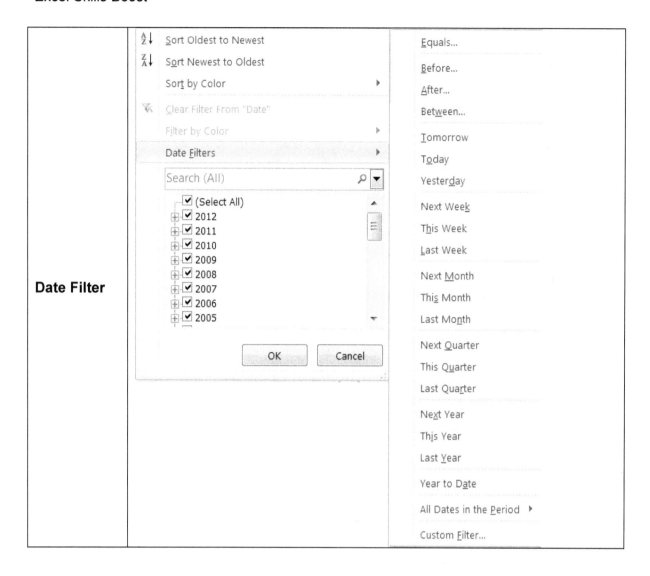

You can also get the **Top 10** option with a **number filter**. Here you can specify either the **Top** or **Bottom** of the range and you can specify any number of items, **not just 10**.

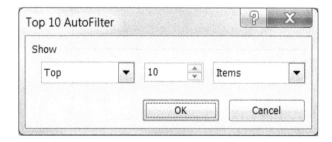

You can also select **Custom** for each type of filter and here you can set your own criteria.

Apply AutoFilter

Method

1. Select any **cell** within the data list you wish to filter
2. From the **Data** tab, in the **Sort & Filter** group, select **Filter**

3. **Drop-down** arrows will appear on each column heading

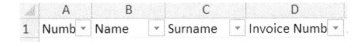

4. Select the **drop-down** arrow in the column you want to filter on
5. Select the **check boxes** for the items you would like to filter

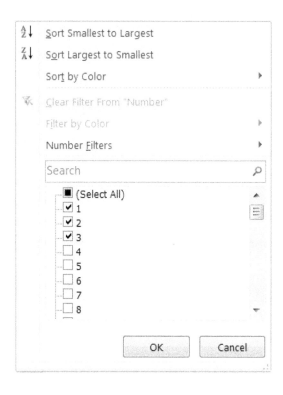

6. Select **OK**

Once you have applied an AutoFilter you can also scroll down the data list and once you have found a cell you would like to filter on you can Right click and filter the list in place:

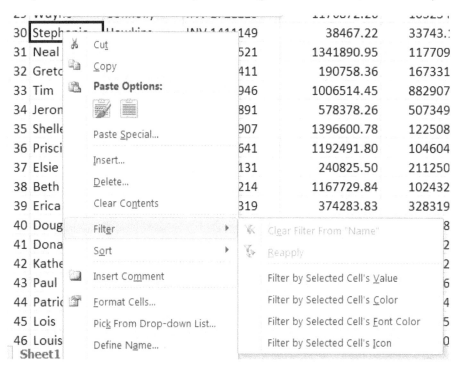

If your data have **blank** rows you can still use it, but you will have to **manually** select all the data *including* the spaces first.

If your data *does not* have **headings AutoFilter** will automatically assume that the first row of data is the headings. To avoid this **manually** add headings or select the data and include one **blank** row above to act as headings.

Once the data is filtered in any way the column that was used will have a different icon and the data row numbers will be in blue. Both of these indicators warn you that you might not be looking at all the data.

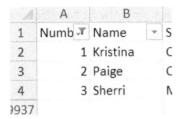

Clear Filter

This will clear the filter from a column or columns.

Method

1. Select the drop-down arrow of a filtered column
2. Select Clear Filter From "[Col]"

OR

1. From the **Data** tab, in the **Sort & Filter** group, select **Clear**

2. This will clear **all** applied filters

Remove AutoFilter

Method

1. From the **Data** tab, in the **Sort & Filter** group, select **Filter**

2. The drop-down arrows will now be removed and all the underlying data will be visible again

Advanced Filter Features

Advanced Filter enables you to set a complex set of criteria on which you can extract certain fields and certain records to another worksheet. It is very useful when you do not want all the columns of the original data extracted.

Advanced Filter is also helpful to extract either unique records or to remove duplicate values.

Method

1. Select the **worksheet** where you would like the data to appear
2. **Copy** the relevant **headings**, with the **criteria** below
3. **Copy** the **headings** where the **extracted** data must **begin**

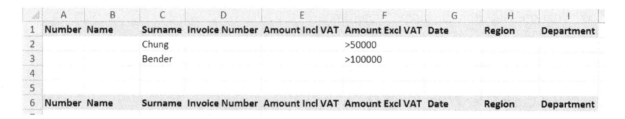

	A	B	C	D	E	F	G	H	I
1	Number	Name	Surname	Invoice Number	Amount Incl VAT	Amount Excl VAT	Date	Region	Department
2			Chung			>50000			
3			Bender			>100000			
4									
5									
6	Number	Name	Surname	Invoice Number	Amount Incl VAT	Amount Excl VAT	Date	Region	Department

4. From the **Data** tab, in the **Sort & Filter** group, select **Advanced**
5. From **Action**, select **Copy to another location**
6. From **List range**, select the **entire list range**, including the **headings** from the **source data**
7. From **Criteria range**, select the **headings** and **criteria**
8. From **Copy to**, select the **copied headings** where the **result** will be placed

9. Select **OK**

Exercise: Filtering Data

Open file: **Filtering Data.xlsx**

Steps

- Select cell **E1** on the **Data** worksheet
- Enter a **SUBTOTAL** function in cell **E1**. You can either type it in or use the **function libraries** and dialog box

function_num	9
ref1	E3:E9937

- The total of **Col E** will now be displayed above the data
- Select cell **F1** on the **Data** worksheet
- Enter a **SUBTOTAL** function in cell **F1**. You can either type it in or use the **function libraries** and dialog box

function_num	9
ref1	F3:F9937

- The total of **Col F** will now be displayed above the data
- Select any cell within the data list. (Say **B15** for example)
- Click on [**Data**][**Sort & Filter**][**Filter**]
- The headings of the data will now have **drop-down** boxes in them
- Apply a **filter** on the **Number** field. Use the [**Number Filters**][**Between...**] option and display data where the **Number** is between **300** and **310**
- You should see the following:

	A	B	C	D	E	F	G
1				Totals	7 404 469.17	6 495 148.39	
2	Number	Name	Surname	Invoice Number	Amount Incl VAT	Amount Excl VAT	Date
302	300	Tiffany	Nash	INV 1547136	898 749.04	788 376.35	01/05/2011
303	301	Todd	Wilkerson	INV 1648520	777 155.17	681 715.06	30/04/2011
304	302	Jill	Kent	INV 1223982	3 432.55	3 011.01	29/04/2011
305	303	Erin	Finch	INV 1153742	169 321.44	148 527.58	28/04/2011
306	304	Melinda	Starr	INV 1342446	1 325 078.80	1 162 349.82	27/04/2011
307	305	Julie	Holland	INV 1991045	423 469.97	371 464.89	26/04/2011
308	306	Stanley	Glover	INV 1717783	1 228 997.49	1 078 067.97	25/04/2011
309	307	Karen	Clements	INV 1383250	519 198.18	455 437.00	24/04/2011
310	308	Judy	Schultz	INV 1384729	1 002 097.77	879 033.13	23/04/2011
311	309	Raymond	Hawley	INV 1385215	2 482.20	2 177.37	22/04/2011
312	310	Julie	Skinner	INV 1938010	1 054 486.56	924 988.21	21/04/2011

- Note that the **Totals** have adjusted due to the **SUBTOTAL** function
- Also, note the change in **drop-down icon** for the **Number** field and that the row numbers are **blue** now

- Click on [**Data**][**Sort & Filter**][**Clear**]
- **All** the data will display again
- Apply a filter on the **Amount Incl VAT** field. Use the [**Number Filters**][**Top 10...**] option and display the **Bottom 5** items
- You should see the following:

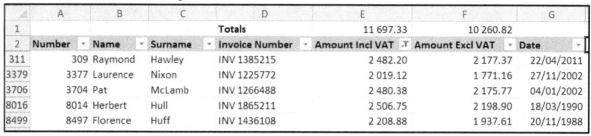

	A	B	C	D	E	F	G
1				Totals	11 697.33	10 260.82	
2	Number	Name	Surname	Invoice Number	Amount Incl VAT	Amount Excl VAT	Date
311	309	Raymond	Hawley	INV 1385215	2 482.20	2 177.37	22/04/2011
3379	3377	Laurence	Nixon	INV 1225772	2 019.12	1 771.16	27/11/2002
3706	3704	Pat	McLamb	INV 1266488	2 480.38	2 175.77	04/01/2002
8016	8014	Herbert	Hull	INV 1865211	2 506.75	2 198.90	18/03/1990
8499	8497	Florence	Huff	INV 1436108	2 208.88	1 937.61	20/11/1988

- Note that the **Totals** have adjusted due to the **SUBTOTAL** function
- Also, note the change in **drop-down icon** for the **Amount Incl VAT** field and that the row numbers are **blue** now
- Click on [**Data**][**Sort & Filter**][**Clear**]
- All the data will display again
- Apply a filter on the Date field. Display the first 10 days of January 2010 (Use the selection boxes)
- You should see the following:

	A	B	C	D	E	F	G
1				Totals	9 889 792.24	8 675 256.35	
2	Number	Name	Surname	Invoice Number	Amount Incl VAT	Amount Excl VAT	Date
778	776	Phyllis	Norton	INV 1861807	1 385 991.68	1 215 782.18	10/01/2010
779	777	Peggy	Blackburn	INV 1803131	1 145 215.62	1 004 575.11	09/01/2010
780	778	Elaine	O'Connell	INV 1332212	515 713.66	452 380.40	08/01/2010
781	779	Jason	Bowling	INV 1749772	391 574.61	343 486.50	07/01/2010
782	780	Neal	Robinson	INV 1475242	565 981.59	496 475.08	06/01/2010
783	781	Diana	Pritchard	INV 1207557	1 423 995.89	1 249 119.20	05/01/2010
784	782	Nina	Lawson	INV 1434516	1 417 434.11	1 243 363.25	04/01/2010
785	783	Maxine	Dickerson	INV 1978876	627 662.62	550 581.25	03/01/2010
786	784	Ted	Livingston	INV 1789392	1 343 562.00	1 178 563.16	02/01/2010
787	785	Allen	Hansen	INV 1941214	1 072 660.46	940 930.23	01/01/2010

- Note that the **Totals** have adjusted due to the **SUBTOTAL** function
- Also, note the change in **drop-down icon** for the **Date** field and that the row numbers are blue now

Exercise: Advanced Filtering

Open file: **Advanced Filtering.xlsx**

We want the filter the data on the data sheet to bring back the following data:

- All sales **after 20 February 2012** *AND*
- All sales from people with a surname **Bender** *AND*
- All sales from people with a name of **Patrick** that are **more than 1000 000**

Steps

- Enter the criteria on the **Advanced Filter** worksheet

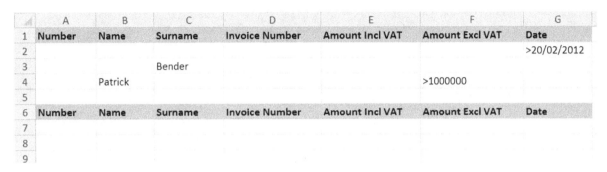

	A	B	C	D	E	F	G
1	Number	Name	Surname	Invoice Number	Amount Incl VAT	Amount Excl VAT	Date
2							>20/02/2012
3			Bender				
4		Patrick				>1000000	
5							
6	Number	Name	Surname	Invoice Number	Amount Incl VAT	Amount Excl VAT	Date
7							
8							
9							

- Each **new criterion** is on a **separate** line
- Make sure your **date format** is the same as your system format (you can check on the original data to see your system format e.g. **DD/MM/YYYY** or **YYYY/MM/DD**)
- Click on **[Data][Sort & Filter][Advanced]**
- Select the following options:

- Select **Copy to another location**
- In the **List range** box, select somewhere in the original data on the **Data** tab and press **Ctrl + A**
- In the **Criteria range** box select the cells **A1:G4** (you must always select the **headings** as well)
- In the **Copy to** box, select the cells **A6:G6**
- Click on **OK**

Excel Skills Boost

Solution

	Number	Name	Surname	Invoice Number	Amount Incl VAT	Amount Excl VAT	Date
1	Number	Name	Surname	Invoice Number	Amount Incl VAT	Amount Excl VAT	Date
2							>20/02/2012
3			Bender				
4		Patrick				>1000000	
5							
6	Number	Name	Surname	Invoice Number	Amount Incl VAT	Amount Excl VAT	Date
7	1	Kristina	Chung	INV 1614589	476 144.56	417 670.67	24/02/2012
8	2	Paige	Chen	INV 1253236	1 084 906.46	951 672.33	23/02/2012
9	3	Sherri	Melton	INV 1095721	113 729.51	99 762.73	22/02/2012
10	4	Gretchen	Hill	INV 1974050	99 620.19	87 386.13	21/02/2012
11	6	Patrick	Song	INV 1681825	1 243 839.80	1 091 087.54	19/02/2012
12	8	Hazel	Bender	INV 1287222	1 382 707.99	1 212 901.75	17/02/2012
13	42	Katherine	Bender	INV 1821220	1 313 883.78	1 152 529.63	14/01/2012
14	359	Leon	Bender	INV 1762101	300 530.81	263 623.52	03/03/2011
15	1634	Patrick	Strauss	INV 1136289	1 406 741.28	1 233 983.58	05/09/2007
16	2076	Patrick	Huffman	INV 1641666	1 492 001.64	1 308 773.37	20/06/2006
17	2756	Patrick	Melton	INV 1349523	1 240 283.42	1 087 967.91	09/08/2004
18	2865	Arthur	Bender	INV 1650664	305 152.00	267 677.19	22/04/2004
19	5502	Eddie	Bender	INV 1856814	1 338 263.32	1 173 915.19	01/02/1997
20	5841	Kerry	Bender	INV 1476320	492 011.32	431 588.88	28/02/1996
21	5999	Patrick	Knowles	INV 1175780	1 253 018.58	1 099 139.11	23/09/1995
22	6283	Kurt	Bender	INV 1776624	1 035 806.23	908 601.96	13/12/1994
23	7944	Patrick	Schwarz	INV 1198323	1 234 745.27	1 083 109.89	27/05/1990
24	8230	Ben	Bender	INV 1378966	286 587.91	251 392.90	14/08/1989
25	9558	Sylvia	Bender	INV 1285222	212 904.76	186 758.56	25/12/1985

Group and Outline

If you have a list of data that you want to group and summarize, you can create an outline of up to eight levels, one for each group. Each inner level, represented by a higher number in the outline symbols displays detail data for the preceding outer level, represented by a lower number in the outline symbols. Use an outline to quickly display summary rows or columns, or to reveal the detail data for each group. You can create an outline of rows, an outline of columns, or an outline of both rows and columns.

Group rows and Columns

Method

1. Select the **rows** or **columns** that contain the detailed data
2. From the **Data** tab, in the **Outline** group, select **Group**

Group

3. **Repeat** the steps above if you want to create more than one group

Ungroup Parts of the Outline

Method

1. Select the **rows** or **columns** that you would like to **ungroup**
2. From the **Data** tab, in the **Outline** group, select **Ungroup**

Ungroup

Remove an Outline

<u>Method</u>

1. Select any **cell** on the **worksheet**
2. From the **Data** tab, in the **Outline** group, select the **drop-down** under **Ungroup**
3. Select **Clear Outline**

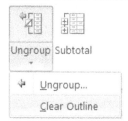

Adding or removing outlines does **not** affect the data on the worksheet.

If you **ungrouped** data in its **summarised** form you may need to **unhide** those rows **afterwards** in order to display them again.

Exercise: Group and Outline

Open file: *Group and Outline.xlsx*

Steps

- Select cells **C4** to **E4**
- Click on [**Data**][**Outline**][**Group**]
- Select **columns**
- Click **OK**
- Select cells **G4** to **I4**
- Click on **F4**
- Select cells **K4** to **M4**
- Click on **F4**
- Select cells **O4** to **Q4**
- Click on **F4**
- Click on the first level (**1**) to **collapse** the table

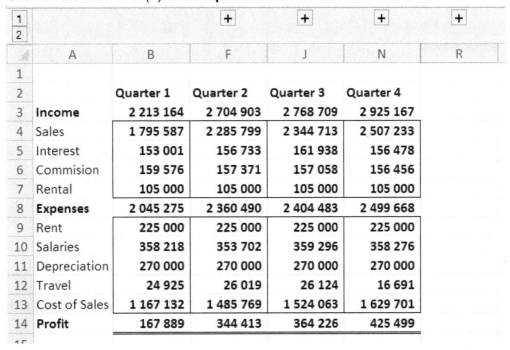

	A	B	F	J	N	R
1						
2		Quarter 1	Quarter 2	Quarter 3	Quarter 4	
3	**Income**	2 213 164	2 704 903	2 768 709	2 925 167	
4	Sales	1 795 587	2 285 799	2 344 713	2 507 233	
5	Interest	153 001	156 733	161 938	156 478	
6	Commision	159 576	157 371	157 058	156 456	
7	Rental	105 000	105 000	105 000	105 000	
8	**Expenses**	2 045 275	2 360 490	2 404 483	2 499 668	
9	Rent	225 000	225 000	225 000	225 000	
10	Salaries	358 218	353 702	359 296	358 276	
11	Depreciation	270 000	270 000	270 000	270 000	
12	Travel	24 925	26 019	26 124	16 691	
13	Cost of Sales	1 167 132	1 485 769	1 524 063	1 629 701	
14	**Profit**	167 889	344 413	364 226	425 499	

- Select cells **B4** to **B7**
- Click on **[Data][Outline][Group]**
- Select **rows**
- Click **OK**
- Select cells **B9** to **B13**
- Click on **F4**
- Click on the first level (**1**) to **collapse** the table

	A	B	F	J	N	R
1						
2		Quarter 1	Quarter 2	Quarter 3	Quarter 4	
3	Income	2 213 164	2 704 903	2 768 709	2 925 167	
8	Expenses	2 045 275	2 360 490	2 404 483	2 499 668	
14	Profit	167 889	344 413	364 226	425 499	

Working with Charts

Charts are used to display series of numeric data in a graphical format to make it easier to understand large quantities of data and the relationship between different series of data.

Excel supports many types of charts to help you display data in ways that are meaningful to your audience. When you create a chart or change an existing chart, you can select from a variety of chart types (such as a column chart or a pie chart) and their subtypes (such as a stacked column chart or a pie, 3-D chart). You can also create a combination chart by using more than one chart type in your chart.

Creating a Chart

To create a chart, you can either use the **Chart Tools** or Press the **F11** key.

The **Chart Tools** are organised in the **Design**, **Layout** and **Format** tabs of the **Chart Ribbon**. By using the **Chart Tools,** you can also create a chart by specifying your own series.

> *You can create a chart from **non-adjacent** data on the worksheet. To do so, select the **first range** of data, and then press the **Ctrl** key while you select **the second range** of data. Press **F11**.*

Method

1. **Select** the data you wish to use in your chart
2. Press **F11**
3. A default chart is created on a new worksheet that you can now **edit**

OR

1. **Select** the data you wish to use in your chart
2. From the **Insert** tab, in the **Charts** group, select the chart type you want

3. A chart is created on the same worksheet that you can **edit**

> *Once you have created a chart and select it, the **Chart Ribbon** will become visible with a **Design**, **Layout** and **Format** tab*

Design Tab

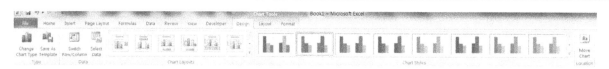

The **Design** tab contains the functionality to:

- Change your chart type
- Switch rows and columns
- Change series
- Apply some built-in chart layouts and chart styles

Layout Tab

The **Layout** tab contains the functionality to:

- Change the layout of the chart
- Change the format
- Add titles
- Add trend lines
- Change chart properties

Format Tab

The **Format** tab contains the functionality to:

- Change the format of your chart

Changing the Chart Type

You might want to change your chart to another chart type.

Method

1. **Right** click on the **Chart Area**
2. From the **Shortcut** menu select **Change Chart Type**

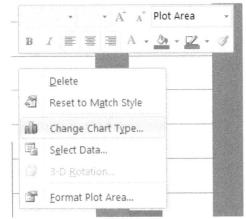

3. Select the new **Chart Type**

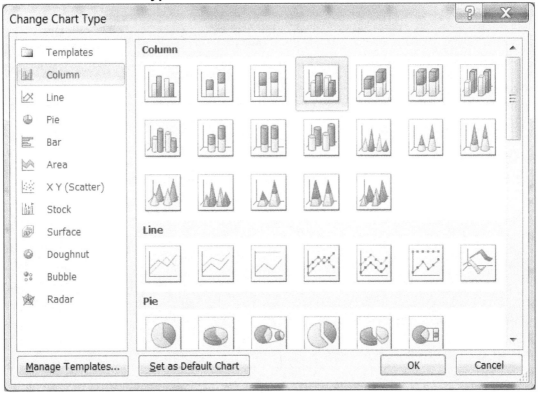

4. Select **OK**

> *You can also change the **Chart Type** from the **Design** tab on the **Chart Ribbon**.*

Changing the Location of a Chart

You can move a chart to an existing worksheet or it can be placed on its own new sheet.

Method

1. **Right** click the **Chart Area**
2. From the **Shortcut** menu select **Move Chart**
3. Select the desired **location**

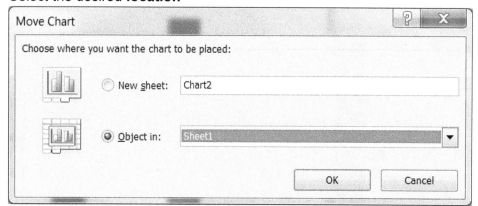

4. Select **OK**

> You can also change the *location* of a chart from the *Design* tab on the *Chart Ribbon*.

Edit Chart Labels

Method

1. Select the **Chart**
2. From the **Layout** tab, in the **Labels** group, select the desired **option**

3. The **Chart** will update **automatically**

Specifying your own Series

If you find that the data is not in sequence or a group of cells, you may need to create your own Series, specifying the labels and values.

Method

1. Select any **blank** cell on the worksheet
2. From the **Insert** tab, in the **Charts** group, select the desired **Chart**

3. A **blank** chart will then appear
4. From the **Design** tab, in the **Data** group, select **Select Data**
5. **Delete** the range in the **Chart data range** area (if there is something there)
6. Select **Add** in the **Legend Entries (Series)** box

7. In the **Series name** box, you can either enter the name or select the red arrow and select the cell for the name of the series
8. In the **Series values** box select the red arrow and select the cells where the values are that you want to chart

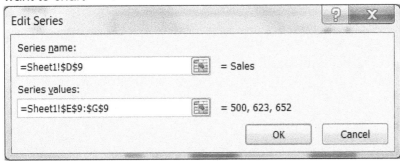

9. Select **OK**
10. Select **Add** again if you are wanting to add another **series**
11. To put **labels** on the **X axis** (Bottom of the chart), select **Edit** in the **Horizontal (Category) Axis Labels**
12. In **the Axis Label Range** box select the **red** arrow
13. Select the **cells** where you have the **X axis** labels e.g. Months, Branches

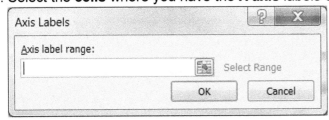

14. Select **OK**, **OK**

Creating a Chart with Two Independent axes

Sometimes you have two sets of data that are very different in their scales. For example, one set of data that are in the millions and another that are in the hundreds. For this kind of graph, you would like two different axes to show.

Method

1. Create you graph the way you would normally e.g. pressing **F11**
2. **Select** the data series of the smaller data set by **clicking** on it in the graph

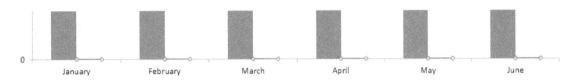

3. **Right** click and select **Format Data Series...**

4. Select **Secondary Axis**, click **Close**

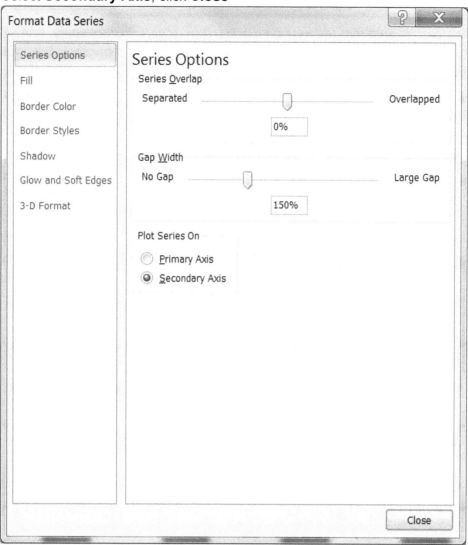

5. On the **Chart Tools Design** tab, Click on **Change Chart Type** in the **Type** group

6. Select **another** chart type e.g. **Line** graph and click **OK**

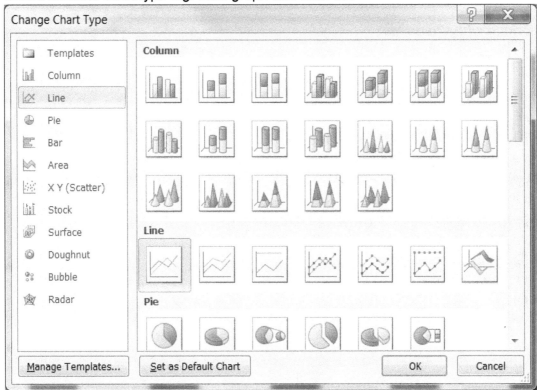

7. You will now have a graph with two different axes

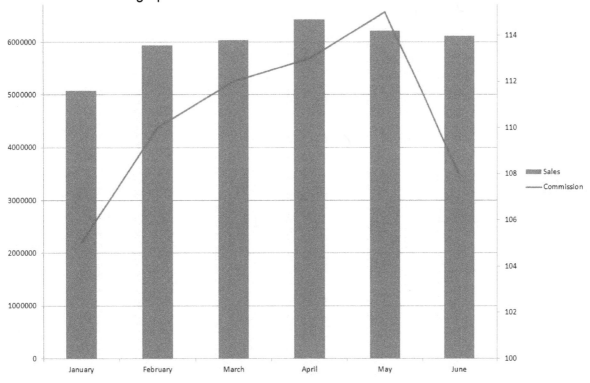

Exercise: Working with Charts

Open file: *Working with Charts.xlsx*

Steps

- Click anywhere in the data on **Sheet1**
- Press **F11**
- Click [**Design**][**Type**][**Change Chart Type**]
- Select a **Line** graph and click **OK**
- **Right** click on the **horizontal axis** (Monday, Tuesday, etc.), select **Format Axis...**
- Select the **Alignment** tab
- Change the **Text direction** to **Rotate all text 270**
- Click on **Close**
- Click [**Design**][**Location**][**Move Chart**]
- Select **Object in Sheet1**
- Click **OK**

Solution

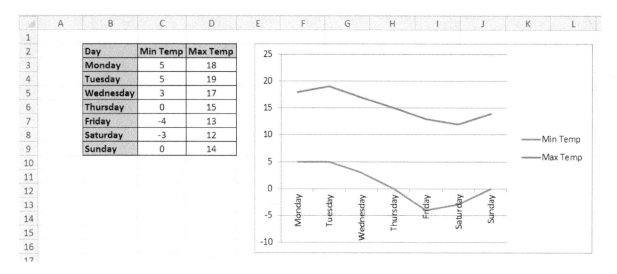

Exercise: Dual Axes

Open file: ***Dual Axes.xlsx***

Steps

- Click anywhere in the data on **Sheet1**
- Press **F11**

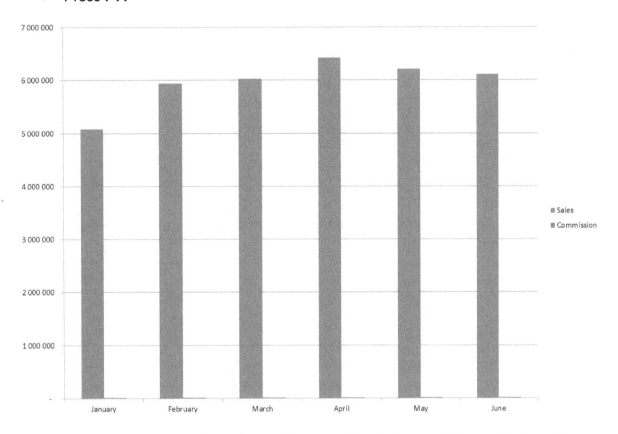

- Select on one of the **Commission** bar and **right** click, select **Format Data Series...**
- Select **Secondary Axis** and click **Close**
- Click **[Design][Type][Change Chart Type]**
- Select a **Line** graph and click **OK**
- Click **[Layout][Labels][Axis Titles][Primary Vertical Axis Title][Horizontal Title]** to add a title for **Sales**

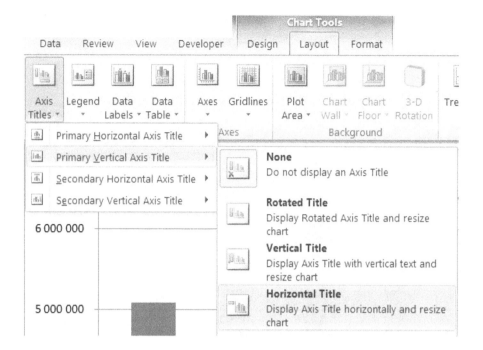

- Rename the title to **Sales**
- Click [**Layout**][**Labels**][**Axis Titles**][**Secondary Vertical Axis Title**][**Horizontal Title**] to add a title for **Commission**
- Rename the title to **Commission**

Solution

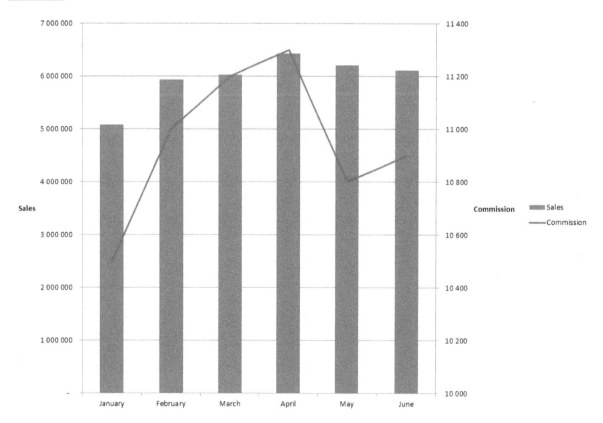

Using comments

You can add notes to a worksheet by using comments. Using comments can help you make a worksheet easier to understand by providing additional context for the data it contains. For example, you can use a comment as a note that provides information about data in an individual cell. You can also add a comment to a column heading to provide guidance on data that a user should enter.

When a cell has a comment, a red indicator appears in the corner of the cell. When you rest the pointer on the cell, the comment appears.

After you add comments, you can edit and format the text in comments, move or resize the comments, copy them, display or hide them, or control how they and their indicators are displayed. When you no longer need comments, you can delete them.

Add a comment

Method

1. Select the cell that you want to add a comment to
2. On the **Review** tab, in the **Comments** group, click **New Comment**

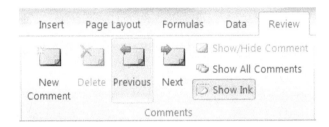

3. In the body of the comment, type the comment text
4. Click outside the comment box

    The comment box disappears, but the comment indicator remains

OR

1. Select the cell that you want to add a comment to
2. **Right click** on your mouse or track pad
3. Select **Insert Comment**
4. In the body of the comment, type the comment text
5. Click outside the comment box

Keyboard shortcut: *You can also press **SHIFT+F2** to **add** or **edit** a comment in a cell.*

Edit a comment

Method

1. Select the cell that contains the comment that you want to edit
2. On the **Review** tab, in the **Comments** group, click **Edit Comment**

3. In the **comment text** box, edit the comment text

OR

1. Select the cell that contains the comment that you want to edit
2. **Right click** on your mouse or track pad
3. Select **Edit Comment**
4. In the comment text box, edit the comment text

Delete a comment

Method

1. Click the cell that contains the comment that you want to delete
2. On the **Review** tab, in the **Comments** group, click **Delete**

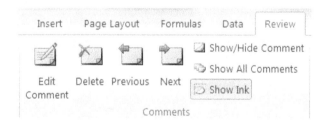

OR

1. Click the cell that contains the comment that you want to delete
2. **Right click** on your mouse or track pad
3. Select **Delete Comment**

Display or hide comments on the worksheet

Method

1. Click the cell or cells that contain a comment indicator
2. On the **Review** tab, in the **Comments** group, click **Show/Hide Comment**

OR

1. Click the cell or cells that contain a comment indicator
2. **Right click** on your mouse or track pad
3. Select **Show/Hide Comments**

Display or hide all comments on the worksheet

Method

1. On the **Review** tab, in the **Comments** group, click **Show All Comments**

2. Clicking **Show All Comments** again will hide all comments on the worksheet

Exercise: Using Comments

Open file: ***Using comments.xlsx***

Steps

- On **Sheet1** is a list of invoices, there are certain **duplicates** (4 duplicates, 8 cells)
- Insert the following comment on cells with the duplicate invoice numbers:

    Please Investigate the duplicate invoices

- Delete the comment on cell **E2**
- Click on [**Review**][**Comments**][**Next**] to cycle through the list of comments

Solution

196	195	35468	15/09/2012 Saturday
197	196	35673	**Joe Soap:** Please Investigate the duplicate invoices.
198	197	35673	
199	198	35776	
200	199	36301	24/12/2012 Monday

Data Validation

You use data validation to control the type of data or the values that users enter into a cell. For example, you may want to restrict data entry to a certain range of dates, limit choices by using a list or make sure that only positive whole numbers are entered.

Data validation is an Excel feature that you can use to define restrictions on what data can or should be entered in a cell. You can configure data validation to prevent users from entering data that is not valid. If you prefer, you can allow users to enter invalid data but warn them when they try to type it in the cell. You can also provide messages to define what input you expect for the cell, and instructions to help users correct any errors.

Data validation is invaluable when you want to share a workbook with others in your organization, and you want the data entered in the workbook to be accurate and consistent.

Among other things, you can use data validation to do the following:

- **Restrict data to predefined items in a list.** For example, you can limit types of departments to Sales, Finance, R&D, and IT. Similarly, you can create a list of values from a range of cells elsewhere in the worksheet.
- **Restrict numbers outside a specified range.** For example, you can specify a minimum limit of deductions to two times the number of children in a particular cell.
- **Restrict dates outside a certain time frame.** For example, you can specify a time frame between today's date and 3 days from today's date.
- **Restrict times outside a certain time frame.** For example, you can specify a time frame for serving breakfast between the time when the restaurant opens and 5 hours after the restaurant opens.
- **Limit the number of text characters.** For example, you can limit the allowed text in a cell to 10 or fewer characters. Similarly, you can set the specific length for a full name field (C1) to be the current length of a first name field (A1) and the last name field (B1), plus 10 characters.
- **Validate data based on formulas or values in other cells.** For example, you can use data validation to set a maximum limit for commissions and bonuses of 3,600, based on the overall projected payroll value. If users enter more than 3,600 in the cell, they see a validation message.

Restrict data entry to values in a drop-down list

Method

1. On a separate worksheet, create the **list** of items you want to use in your drop-down list

2. Create the **form** you would like people to complete on a different worksheet

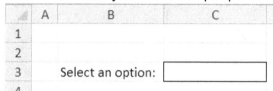

3. Select the **cell** where you want the drop-down box to appear (**C3** in this example)

4. From the **Data** tab, in the **Data Tools** group, select **Data Validation**

5. On the **Data Validation** dialog box, under the **Settings** tab

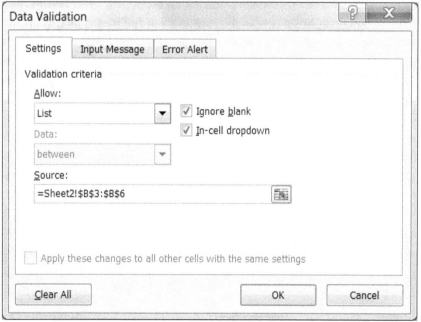

6. In the **Allow** box, select **List** by clicking on the **drop-down** arrow

7. Click on the **red arrow** under the **Source** box, select the list of data you created earlier

8. Select **OK**
9. You can now select the needed value from a **drop-down** list

◢	A	B	C
1			
2			
3		Select an option:	
4			Apples
5			Pears
			Oranges
6			Bananas

*If you **copy** and **paste** cell C3, the new cell will also have the drop-down list available*

You can also validate the value of the cell in other ways as described above. You can get these options by selecting other values from the **Allow** drop-down list.

Select an Input message for the Data Validation

You can choose to show an input message when the user selects the cell. Input messages are generally used to offer users guidance about the type of data that you want to be entered in the cell. This type of message appears near the cell. You can move this message if you want to, and it remains until you move to another cell or press ESC.

Method

1. Follow Steps **1 to 7** above
2. Select the **Input Message** tab on the **Data Validation** Dialog box

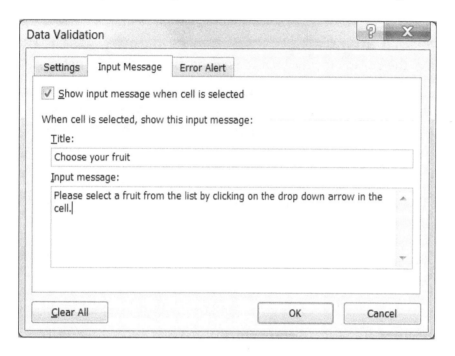

3. Enter a **Title** and **Input message** to display
4. Click **OK**
5. Your **Input Message** will now appear when you **select** the cell

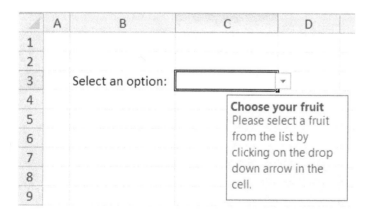

Select an Error Alert for the Data Validation

You can also choose to show an error alert that appears only after users enter invalid data.

Method

1. Follow Steps **1 to 7** above
2. Select the **Error Alert** tab on the **Data Validation** Dialog box

3. Enter a **Title** and **Error message** to display
4. From the **Style** drop-down list select a **style** of error message to display
5. Click **OK**
6. Your **Error Message** will now appear when you enter **incorrect** data in the cell

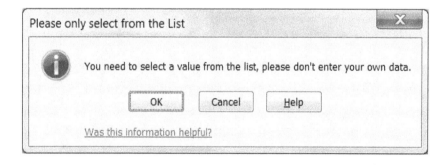

Exercise: Data Validation

Open file: ***Data Validation.xlsx***

Steps

- Select **Sheet2**
- Select the data range (**B3:B10**)
- Click [**Formulas**][**Defined Names**][**Create from selection**]
- Select **Top row**
- Click **OK**
- Select **Sheet1**
- Select cell **C3**
- Click [**Data**][**Data Tools**][**Data Validation**]
- **Allow** a **List**
- In the **Source** box, click **F3** and select **Ratings**
- You should now be able to select a rating from the **drop-down** list in the cell

Solution

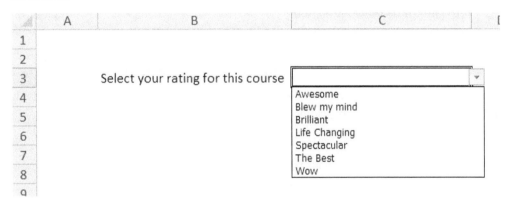

Goal Seek

If you know the result that you want from a formula, but are not sure what input value the formula needs to get that result, use the Goal Seek feature. For example, suppose that you need to borrow some money. You know how much money you want, how long you want to take to pay off the loan, and how much you can afford to pay each month. You can use Goal Seek to determine what interest rate you will need to secure in order to meet your loan goal. Goal Seek works only with one variable input value.

Method

1. Create a formula you want to evaluate, e.g. the **PMT** formula

   For a formula like **PMT**, where you get the payments on a loan, it would not be easy to determine the loan amount if you know the payment you could afford. Goal Seek allows you to find this amount for example.

2. From the **Data** tab, in the **Data Tools** group, select the **drop-down** under the **What-if Analysis** button and click on **Goal seek...**

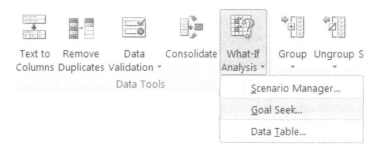

3. In the **Goal Seek** dialog box, select the value you would like to **change** in the **Set cell** box

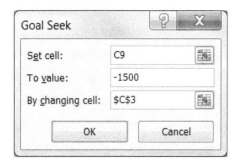

4. Type the value you would like that cell to be in the **To value** box
5. Select the variable you would like to change in order to get your result in the **By changing cell** box
6. Select **OK**
7. A **Goal Seek Status** dialog box will now appear

Amount borrowed	73 977.65
Interest Rate	8.00%
Term (months)	60
PMT	-1 500.00

Goal Seek Status

Goal Seeking with Cell C9 found a solution.

Target value: -1500
Current value: -1 500.00

OK   Cancel

Step

Pause

8. If you want to **accept** the new value as calculated by Excel, select **OK**
9. If you do **not** want to **accept** the new value, click on **Cancel**

Exercise: Goal Seek

Open file: *Goal Seek.xlsx*

Steps

- **Sheet1** contains a **PMT** formula and gives you a **payment** for a loan of 300 000, over 60 months at an interest rate of 8% (-6 082.92)
- Select cell **C10**
- Click on **[Data][Data Tools][What-if Analysis][Goal Seek...]**
- On the **Goal Seek** Dialog box:

  Set cell: **C10**
  To value: **-4500**
  By changing cell: **$C$4**

- Click **OK**
- Click **OK** on the **Goal Seek Status** dialog box
- You will now have a **new** loan amount that will give you a payment of **4 500**

Solution

▲	A	B	C
1			
2		**PMT Formula**	
3			
4		**Amount borrowed**	221 932.95
5			
6		**Interest Rate**	8.00%
7			
8		**Term (months)**	60
9			
10		**PMT**	-4 500.00
11			

Macros

To automate a repetitive task, you can quickly record a macro in Excel. You can also create a macro by using the Visual Basic Editor in Visual Basic for Applications (VBA) to write your own macro script or to copy all or part of a macro to a new macro. After you create a macro, you can assign it to an object (such as a toolbar button, graphic, or control) so that you can run it by clicking the object. If you no longer use a macro, you can delete it.

Record a Macro

When you record a macro, the macro recorder records all the steps required to complete the actions that you want your macro to perform. Navigation on the Ribbon is not included in the recorded steps.

Method

1. On the **View** tab, in the **Macros** group, click on the **drop-down** arrow and select **Record Macro…**

   You can also click on the **record macro icon** on the **status bar** Ready

2. In the **Macro name** box, enter a name for the macro

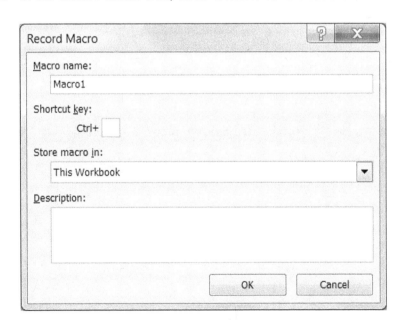

   The first character of the macro name must be a letter. Subsequent characters can be letters, numbers, or underscore characters. **Spaces cannot be used** in a macro name; an underscore character works well as a word separator. If you use a macro name that is also a cell reference, you may get an error message that the macro name is not valid

3. To assign a **Ctrl** combination shortcut key to run the macro, in the **Shortcut key** box, type any lowercase letter or uppercase letter that you want to use

    The shortcut key will override any equivalent default Excel shortcut key while the workbook that contains the macro is open

4. In the **Store macro in** list, select the workbook where you want to store the macro

    If you want a macro to be available whenever you use Excel, select **Personal Macro Workbook**

5. In the **Description** box, type a description of the macro
6. Click **OK** to start recording
7. Perform the actions that you want to record
8. Click **Stop Recording** Ready ▪ on the left side of the status bar

    OR

    On the **View** tab, in the **Macros** group, click on the **drop-down** arrow and select **Stop Recording**

Run, Edit or Delete a Macro

Method

1. On the **View** tab, in the **Macros** group, click on the **drop-down** arrow and select View Macros

2. The macro dialog box appears displaying all macros created

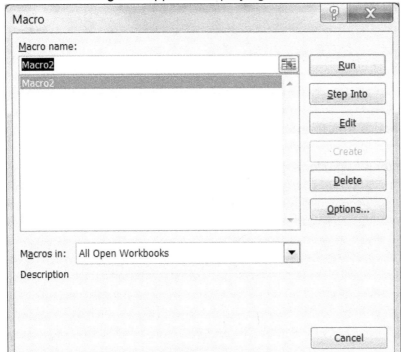

3. Select the macro you wish to **run**, **edit** or **delete**
4. Select **Run**, **Edit** or **Delete**

*You can also view a list of macros by pressing **Alt+F8***

Assign a macro to an object, graphic, or control

Method

1. On a worksheet, right-click the object, graphic, or control to which you want to assign an existing macro, and then click **Assign Macro**
2. In the **Macro name** box, click the macro that you want to assign

Relative Macro

Unless you specify that a macro must be relative, it will run at the exact point when you recorded it. If you want to macro to run in whatever cell is selected, you must make the macro relative.

Method

1. On the **View** tab, in the **Macros** group, click on the **drop-down** arrow and select **Record Macro...**

You can also click on the **record macro icon** on the **status bar** Ready ▢

2. In the **Macro name** box, enter a name for the macro

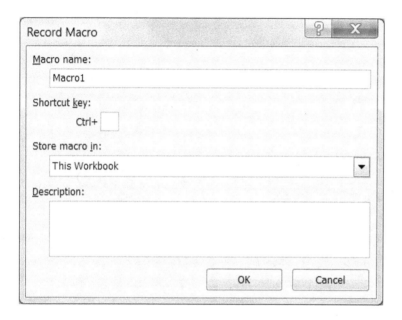

3. In the **Store macro in** list, select the workbook where you want to store the macro
4. In the **Description** box, type a description of the macro
5. Click **OK** to start recording
6. On the **View** tab, in the **Macros** group, click on the **drop-down** arrow and select **Use Relative References** button

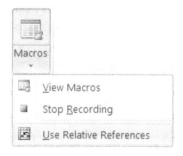

7. Perform the actions that you want to record
8. Click **Stop Recording** Ready ▢ on the left side of the status bar

OR

On the **View** tab, in the **Macros** group, click on the **drop-down** arrow and select **Stop Recording**

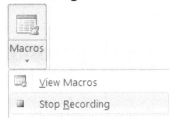

Assign Macros to the Quick Access Toolbar

It is much quicker to access a function to the Quick Access Toolbar or keyboard than having to browse through a number of menu items to select the one you need. So to have quicker access to run a macro you can assign it to the Quick Access Toolbar.

Method

1. Open the Workbook that contains the macro
2. Select the **drop-down** arrow at the end of the **Quick Access Toolbar**

3. Select **More Commands…**
4. Select the **Choose commands from** drop-down and select **Macros** from the list

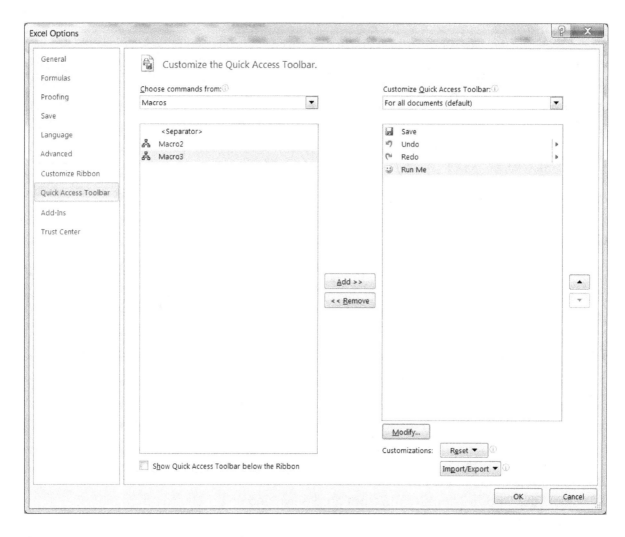

5. Select the macro you want to add from the command list
6. Select the **Add >>** button. The command will be added to the **Quick Access Toolbar** command list
7. Select this **new** command
8. Select the **Modify...** button

9. Select a Symbol and change the Display name

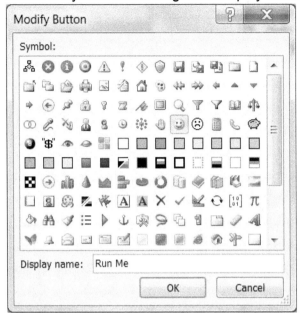

10. Select **OK**, **OK**

> *When you save a workbook that contains a macro you need to save it as a **macro enabled workbook** (**.xlsm** file extension). And when you open this workbook again you need to **enable** the macros. This is done for security, **DO NOT ENABLE MACROS ON A FILE YOU RECEIVED UNLESS YOU ARE 100% SURE ABOUT ITS CONTENT. VIRUSES CAN BE SPREAD THIS WAY**.*

Exercise: Macros

Open file: **Macros.xlsx**

Steps

- Select cell **B4** on **Sheet1**
- Click on the **Macro Record** button

- Enter the **Macro name** as **MySig**

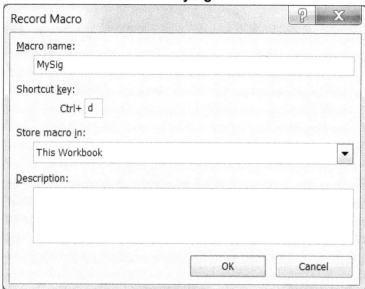

- Enter the lowercase letter **d** next to the **Ctrl +**
- Click on **OK**
- Click on [**View**][**Macros**][**Use Relative References**]
- Enter data as follow on the screen (use your own contact details and required formatting)

	A	B	C
1			
2			
3			
4		Joe Soap	
5		ABC Inc.	
6			
7		Jsoap@abc.com	
8		+44 253 555 6645	

- Click on the Stop Macro recording button when you are done

- Select any empty cell and press **Crtl+d**, your macro should now repeat your signature in the cell you selected

- Click the **drop-down** arrow next to the **Quick Access** tool bar, select **More Commands…**

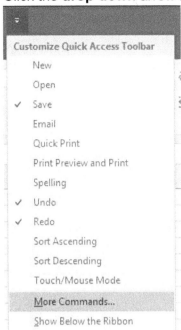

- Select **Macros** from the **Choose commands from** drop-down list

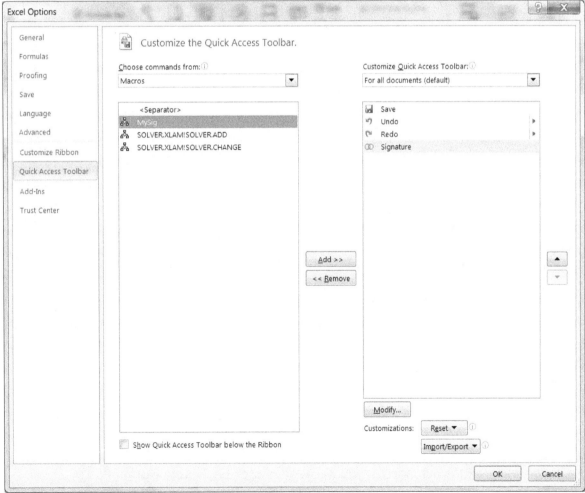

- Select your **MySig** macro and click on **Add>>**
- Click on the **Modify…** button

- Select a **new icon** and change the display name to **Signature**, click **OK**, **OK**
- When you click on the new icon in the Quick Access toolbar your macro will also run

	A	B	C
1			
2		Joe Soap	
3		ABC Inc.	
4			
5		Jsoap@abc.com	
6		+44 253 555 6645	

- Click on **File, Save as…**
- Select **Excel Macro-Enabled Workbook** from the **Save as type** drop-down list

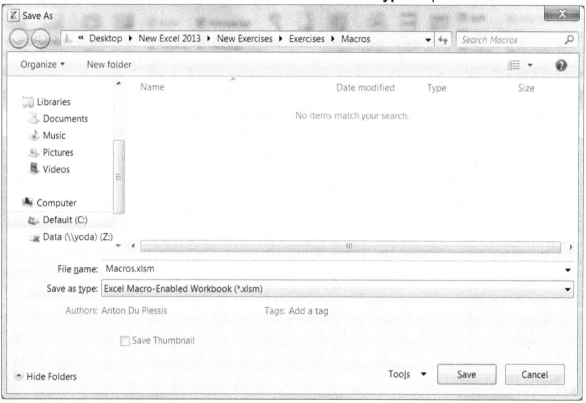

- Click on Save and close the file
- Open the new file you have created
- When you open a macro enabled workbook you will get the following message

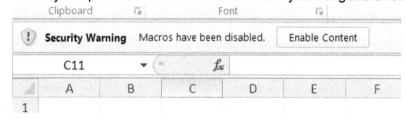

- If you want to run your macros, you will need to click on **Enable Content**

DON'T CLICK ENABLE CONTENT IF YOU <u>DO NOT KNOW</u> WHAT MACROS ARE ON THE FILE

Excel Keyboard Shortcuts - Ctrl combination shortcut keys

Key	Description
CTRL+PgUp	Switches between worksheet tabs, from left-to-right
CTRL+PgDn	Switches between worksheet tabs, from right-to-left
CTRL+SHIFT+(	Un-hides hidden rows within the selection
CTRL+SHIFT+&	Applies outline border to selected cells
CTRL+SHIFT&_	Removes outline border from selected cells
CTRL+SHIFT+~	Applies General number format
CTRL+SHIFT+$	Applies Currency format with two decimal places (negative numbers in parentheses)
CTRL+SHIFT+%	Applies Percentage format with no decimal places
CTRL+SHIFT+^	Applies Scientific number format with two decimal places
CTRL+SHIFT+#	Applies Date format with day, month, and year
CTRL+SHIFT+@	Applies Time format with the hour and minute, and AM or PM
CTRL+SHIFT+!	Applies Number format with two decimal places, thousands separator, and minus sign (-) for negative values
CTRL+SHIFT+*	Selects current region around active cells. In PivotTables, it selects entire PivotTable reports
CTRL+SHIFT+:	Enters the current time
CTRL+`	Alternates between displaying cell values and displaying formulas
CTRL+SHIFT+"	Copies value from cell above an active cell into the cell or the Formula Bar
CTRL+SHIFT+Plus (+)	Displays Insert dialog box to insert blank cells
CTRL+Minus (-)	Displays Delete dialog box to delete selected cells
CTRL+;	Enters current date
CTRL+'	Copies a formula from the cell above the active cell into the cell or the Formula Bar
CTRL+1	Displays Format Cells dialog box
CTRL+2	Applies or removes bold formatting
CTRL+3	Applies or removes italic formatting
CTRL+4	Applies or removes underlining
CTRL+5	Applies or removes strikethrough
CTRL+6	Alternates between hiding and displaying objects
CTRL+8	Displays or hides the outline symbols
CTRL+9	Hides selected rows
CTRL+0	Hides the selected columns
CTRL+A	Selects entire worksheet

Key	Description
CTRL+SHIFT+A	Inserts argument names and parentheses when insertion point is to the right of function names in formulas
CTRL+B	Applies or removes bold formatting
CTRL+C	Copies selected cells
CTRL+D	Uses Fill Down command to copy the contents and format of the topmost cell of a selected range into the cells below
CTRL+F	Displays Find and Replace dialog box, with the Find tab selected
CTRL+SHIFT+F	Opens Format Cells dialog box with the Font tab selected
CTRL+G	Displays Go To dialog box
CTRL+H	Displays Find and Replace dialog box, with Replace tab selected
CTRL+I	Applies or removes italic formatting
CTRL+K	Displays Insert Hyperlink dialog box for new hyperlinks or Edit Hyperlink dialog box for selected existing hyperlinks
CTRL+L	Displays Create Table dialog box
CTRL+N	Creates a new, blank workbook
CTRL+O	Displays Open dialog box to open or find a file
CTRL+SHIFT+O	Selects all cells that contain comments
CTRL+P	Displays Print tab in Microsoft Office Backstage view
CTRL+SHIFT+P	Opens Format Cells dialog box with the Font tab selected
CTRL+R	Uses Fill Right command to copy the contents and format of the leftmost cell of a selected range into the cells to the right
CTRL+S	Saves the active file with its current file name, location, and file format
CTRL+T	Displays Create Table dialog box
CTRL+U	Applies or removes underlining
CTRL+SHIFT+U	Switches between expanding and collapsing of the formula bar
CTRL+V	Inserts contents of the Clipboard at the insertion point and replaces any selection. Available only after cutting or copying an object, text, or cell contents
CTRL+ALT+V	Displays Paste Special dialog box. Available only after cutting or copying an object, text, or cell contents on a worksheet or in another program
CTRL+W	Closes selected workbook window
CTRL+X	Cuts selected cells
CTRL+Y	Repeats last command or action, if possible
CTRL+Z	Uses Undo command to reverse the last command or to delete the last entry that you typed

NOTE: The CTRL combinations **CTRL+E**, **CTRL+J**, **CTRL+M**, and **CTRL+Q** are currently unassigned shortcuts

Excel Keyboard Shortcuts - Function keys

Key	Description
F1	Displays the Excel Help task pane CTRL+F1 displays or hides the ribbon ALT+F1 creates an embedded chart of the data in the current range ALT+SHIFT+F1 inserts a new worksheet
F2	Edits the active cell and positions the insertion point at the end of the cell contents. It also moves the insertion point into the Formula Bar when editing in a cell is turned off. SHIFT+F2 adds or edits a cell comment CTRL+F2 displays the print preview area on the Print tab in the Backstage view
F3	Displays the Paste Name dialog box. Available only if there are existing names in the workbook. SHIFT+F3 displays the Insert Function dialog box
F4	Repeats the last command or action, if possible When a cell reference is selected in a formula, F4 cycles through all the various combinations of absolute and relative references. CTRL+F4 closes the selected workbook window ALT+F4 closes Excel
F5	Displays the Go To dialog box CTRL+F5 restores the window size of the selected workbook window
F6	Switches between the worksheet, ribbon, task pane, and Zoom controls. In a worksheet that has been split (View menu, Manage This Window, Freeze Panes, Split Window command), F6 includes the split panes when switching between panes and the ribbon area. SHIFT+F6 switches between the worksheet, Zoom controls, task pane, and ribbon CTRL+F6 switches to the next workbook window when more than one workbook window is open
F7	Displays the Spelling dialog box to check spelling in the active worksheet or selected range CTRL+F7 performs the Move command on the workbook window when it is not maximized. Use the arrow keys to move the window, and when finished press ENTER or ESC to cancel

Key	Description
F8	Turns extend mode on or off. In extend mode, Extended Selection appears in the status line, and the arrow keys extend the selection SHIFT+8 enables you to add a nonadjacent cell or range to a selection of cells by using the arrow keys CTRL+F8 performs the Size command (on the Control menu for the workbook window) when a workbook is not maximized ALT+F8 displays the Macro dialog box to create, run, edit, or delete a macro
F9	Calculates all worksheets in all open workbooks SHIFT+F9 calculates the active worksheet CTRL+ALT+F9 calculates all worksheets in all open workbooks, regardless of whether they have changed since the last calculation CTRL+ALT+SHIFT+F9 rechecks dependent formulas and then calculates all cells in all open workbooks, including cells not marked as needing to be calculated CTRL+F9 minimizes a workbook window to an icon
F10	Turns key tips on or off. (Pressing ALT does the same thing.) SHIFT+F10 displays the shortcut menu for a selected item ALT+SHIFT+F10 displays the menu or message for an Error Checking button CTRL+F10 maximizes or restores the selected workbook window
F11	Creates a chart of the data in the current range in a separate Chart sheet SHIFT+F11 inserts a new worksheet ALT+F11 opens the Microsoft Visual Basic for Applications Editor, in which you can create a macro by using Visual Basic for Applications (VBA)
F12	Displays the Save As dialog box

Excel Keyboard Shortcuts - Miscellaneous

Key	Description
ESC	Cancels an entry in the cell or Formula Bar Closes an open menu or submenu, dialog box, or message window It also closes full-screen mode when this mode has been applied and returns to normal screen mode to display the ribbon and status bar again
BACKSPACE	Deletes one character to the left in the Formula Bar Also clears the content of the active cell In cell editing mode, it deletes the character to the left of the insertion point
DELETE	Removes the cell contents (data and formulas) from selected cells without affecting cell formats or comments In cell editing mode, it deletes the character to the right of the insertion point
HOME	Moves to the beginning of a row in a worksheet Moves to the cell in the upper-left corner of the window when SCROLL LOCK is turned on Selects the first command on the menu when a menu or submenu is visible CTRL+HOME moves to the beginning of a worksheet CTRL+SHIFT+HOME extends the selection of cells to the beginning of the worksheet
END	END turns End mode on. In End mode, you can then press an arrow key to move to the next nonblank cell in the same column or row as the active cell. If the cells are blank, pressing END followed by an arrow key moves to the last cell in the row or column. END also selects the last command on the menu when a menu or submenu is visible CTRL+END moves to the last cell on a worksheet, to the lowest used row of the rightmost used column. If the cursor is in the formula bar, CTRL+END moves the cursor to the end of the text CTRL+SHIFT+END extends the selection of cells to the last used cell on the worksheet (lower-right corner). If the cursor is in the formula bar, CTRL+SHIFT+END selects all text in the formula bar from the cursor position to the end—this does not affect the height of the formula bar.

Key	Description
PAGE UP	Moves one screen up in a worksheet ALT+PAGE UP moves one screen to the left in a worksheet CTRL+PAGE UP moves to the previous sheet in a workbook CTRL+SHIFT+PAGE UP selects the current and previous sheet in a workbook
PAGE DOWN	Moves one screen down in a worksheet ALT+PAGE DOWN moves one screen to the right in a worksheet CTRL+PAGE DOWN moves to the next sheet in a workbook CTRL+SHIFT+PAGE DOWN selects the current and next sheet in a workbook
ARROW KEYS	Move one cell up, down, left, or right in a worksheet. CTRL+ARROW KEY moves to the edge of the current data region in a worksheet. SHIFT+ARROW KEY extends the selection of cells by one cell CTRL+SHIFT+ARROW KEY extends the selection of cells to the last nonblank cell in the same column or row as the active cell, or if the next cell is blank, extends the selection to the next nonblank cell. LEFT ARROW or RIGHT ARROW selects the tab to the left or right when the ribbon is selected. When a submenu is open or selected, these arrow keys switch between the main menu and the submenu. When a ribbon tab is selected, these keys navigate the tab buttons. DOWN ARROW or UP ARROW selects the next or previous command when a menu or submenu is open. When a ribbon tab is selected, these keys navigate up or down the tab group. DOWN ARROW or ALT+DOWN ARROW opens a selected drop-down list.
ENTER	Completes a cell entry from the cell or the Formula Bar, and selects the cell below (by default). In a data form, it moves to the first field in the next record. Opens a selected menu (press F10 to activate the menu bar) or performs the action for a selected command. ALT+ENTER starts a new line in the same cell CTRL+ENTER fills the selected cell range with the current entry SHIFT+ENTER completes a cell entry and selects the cell above

Key	Description
SPACEBAR	In a dialog box, performs the action for the selected button, or selects or clears a check box. CTRL+SPACEBAR selects an entire column in a worksheet SHIFT+SPACEBAR selects an entire row in a worksheet CTRL+SHIFT+SPACEBAR selects the entire worksheet • If the worksheet contains data, CTRL+SHIFT+SPACEBAR selects the current region. Pressing CTRL+SHIFT+SPACEBAR a second time selects the current region and its summary rows. Pressing CTRL+SHIFT+SPACEBAR a third time selects the entire worksheet. • When an object is selected, CTRL+SHIFT+SPACEBAR selects all objects on a worksheet. ALT+SPACEBAR displays the Control menu for the Excel window
TAB	Moves one cell to the right in a worksheet Moves between unlocked cells in a protected worksheet Moves to the next option or option group in a dialog box SHIFT+TAB moves to the previous cell in a worksheet or the previous option in a dialog box CTRL+TAB switches to the next tab in dialog box CTRL+SHIFT+TAB switches to the previous tab in a dialog box

www.ingramcontent.com/pod-product-compliance
Lightning Source LLC
LaVergne TN
LVHW060140070326
832902LV00018B/2871